Codependency

Explore the Roots of Your Behavior and
Learn to Balance Your Needs.
Borderline Personality Disorder
Management, Learn How to Deal with a
Narcissistic Personality and Escape
from a Codependent Relationship.
Recognize the Signs of a Toxic
Relationship Unmask

Mike Atchigan

Codependency

Mike Atchigan| © Copyright 2021 All Rights Reserved

TABLE OF CONTENTS

TABLE OF CONTENTS _____ 4

INTRODUCTION to codependency _____ 6
    Why then continue?_____ 10

Codependent Personality _____ 14
    General characteristics of the personality with emotional
    dependence _____ 15

The signs of codependency _____ 23
    Where to start? _____ 25

codependency and anxiety _____ 30
    Affective dependence, anxious traits and attachment style ___ 34

codependent personality disorder _____ 38
    Romantic love or emotional addiction?_____ 39
    Interpersonal cycles in emotional dependence_____ 42
    Affective addiction and personality disorders _____ 44

codependent behaviors_____ 47
    The types of emotional employees _____ 54
    Cognitive - Behavioral Therapy for Affective Addiction_____ 55

Codependency and family_____ 58
    The childhood trauma have long-lasting effects _____ 58
    Parent-child addiction _____ 64
    The factory of complacency: how a pathological narcissistic
    parent raises future codependents _____ 66

Strategies for increasing your self-esteem_____ 73
    THE CONCEPT OF SELF-ESTEEM_____ 75
    DIMENSIONALITY OF THE CONCEPT OF SELF-ESTEEM_____ 77
    The importance of having self-esteem _____ 83
    5 things you need to know to have self-esteem _____ 88
    Questions and answers on self-esteem _____ 98

codependency recovery plan_____ 102

HOW TO GET OUT WITH PSYCHODYNAMIC PSYCHOTHERAPY_ 108
HOW TO FREE YOURSELF FROM THE CHAINS OF AFFECTIVE
DEPENDENCE AND BECOME EMOTIONALLY INDEPENDENT __ 111
How to love yourself: who knows you best? _____ 123

Start to Love _____ **132**

Conclusion _____ **142**

INTRODUCTION TO CODEPENDENCY

Despite the absence of real diagnostic criteria with which to identify an Affective Addiction, differentiating it from the more common phenomenon of human love, it will be interesting to observe how the psychotherapists' studies are crowding with individuals (men and women) who present all the symptoms of more serious amorous torment. A torment, however, which in love does not seem to be well founded.

If before today the phenomena of depression and those of compulsive possessiveness, eating disorders (bulimia and anorexia), panic attacks, sexual dysfunctions and disorders, occupied the vast majority of the working hours of a therapist, today just a number considerable number of cases seem to refer to a state of real dependence; only that instead of being attributable to a substance (alcohol, drugs or medicines) or to a behavior (playing cards, dice, horses, etc.), it is attributable to a person; often, even if not always and not necessarily, unattainable for him or her who depends on it.

And what strikes the clinician, in all these cases, it is not so much the absolute patient's inability to escape to a report that he himself is able to recognize hopeless, unsatisfactory, humiliating and often self-destructive, but also the severity of the phenomena which are the background to this: generalized anxiety, depression, insomnia, inappetence, melancholy, fixation of thought.

Certainly many of these manifestations are typical of the vicissitudes of love but, as we shall see, it is precisely the frame of reference that is absent: and where it is not legitimate to speak of love, we are then in the presence of an Affective Dependence.

As can be deduced from this brief introduction, everything refers to the possibility and ability to distinguish between phenomena that only apparently seem similar, but which underlie mechanisms of a very different nature. On the one hand, human love, as a manifestation by an individual to transcend himself and, together with another, to create a new and different reality from the one previously existing. On the other hand, affective dependence, as a manifestation by another individual of being stuck in himself and in his own pain, because it is entangled in a dynamic symbolically identical to that which in the past has fixed or conditioned his growth.

The simplicity of the definition, however, must not be misleading: because on the surface the two phenomena appear really similar and the distinctions are not always as clear and marked as one might expect. It may even happen that the two phenomena at times, even if only minimally, overlap, making it difficult to identify possible solutions.

Love free gift and the egoic core

To orient ourselves, however, we must refer to a concept that is as exhaustive as possible, but at the same time elastic, of love. What is it loved? Or rather, rather than asking ourselves about its nature - something that has always been better for storytellers and poets - we can ask ourselves: in what conditions does it happen? What are the psychic requirements that allow men and women to have this extraordinary experience of self-transcending?

Personally, even without any claim to have read and elaborated everything that has been written on the theme of love, to illustrate these conditions I usually refer to two main texts: one is "The meaning of love" by the Russian philosopher Vladimir Solov'ev; the other is "Illusions of love" by the psychoanalyst Jole Baldaro Verde.

According to the latter, only those who reach genital maturity (in the psychoanalytic sense) can be able to create a real relationship of love. That is, those who have happily passed all the previous stages of the evolutionary process and are therefore able to provide for themselves in all respects, to be autonomous in their choices, capable of making decisions, satisfied with a job that ensures them not only their survival, but also gratification and success. "The genital couple - writes J. B. Verde - is represented by two people who have the entire universe as an object of love, attracted by every new thing, enriched by every encounter, and who do not need to create around themselves a prison made of rigid rules into which they must adapt. Their security comes, paradoxically, from accepting insecurity, ambivalence, risk. Two people for whom fidelity is not a duty, a commitment, one of the walls of the "security prison " but is a choice renewed every day, a free gift that is given to another who responds equally freely. "

Which refers to the considerations of V. Solov'ev for which love is the only force in the world capable of extirpating the egoic nucleus of every single individual, man or woman, and, dragging them beyond itself. Themselves, to make him realize a real, authentic transcendence.

It will be interesting to observe, at this point, that in order for the core to be transcended it must first necessarily exist. It must have formed and consolidated within the human soul in such a way as to offer stability, autonomy, security and last but not least trust and joy of living. Only what exists can then be overcome and indeed transcended in an experience - that of love - which is a further and more significant stage in the human evolutionary process.

It is thanks to the existence of this core that, in healthy love, it is possible to give oneself without the fear of getting lost, to abandon oneself without opposing, to entrust oneself without resisting. Only those who are strong - says the ancient wisdom of the Tao - can yield, only those who are elastic can flex without breaking, only those who possess themselves can give themselves entirely and without any reserve.

And only those who have conquered this inner center are able to serenely evaluate the specific meaning of their own experience of love; and - perhaps with extreme pain - to renounce it where this, for whatever reason, proves limited and limiting, harmful, humiliating or even destructive. Because the love inherent objective, as a human experience, it is still one of growth and the ego expansion, and ultimately, the pleasure and joy of living. Always! Even when it encounters insurmountable obstacles such as illness or death. Because in its deepest nature it should have promoted the intimate agreement between two people, a similar vision of the reality of the world, complicity, friendship, and a sense of mutual belongs. All these things, which although suddenly failing, and while sinking the ego of those who remain in the atrocious pain of loss, nevertheless should have left them enriched with an experience that if on the one hand it may seem unique, on the other hand it is repeatable. That of knowing how to love.

As naive as it may seem to our cynical eyes of modern men, think carefully and agree that in order to really talk about love between two people there should be reciprocity of attention, respect, esteem, desire and trust translated into an experience of joy. Daily. Out of such a context there are only Illusions of love (just to quote JB Verde once again), many of which then decay into real Affective Addictions.Some fundamental questions that I have learned to ask to those who turn to me to heal a supposed wound of love, are those related to the description of their partner and the experiences lived together. Almost always there is incompatibility of soul, lack of respect, different if not opposing projects, needs and desires that cannot be shared. And few, if not absent, were the moments of profound communion and mutual satisfaction.

WHY THEN CONTINUE?

Why torment yourself in the hope that things might change when the supposed change was only desired, dreamed, imagined but never experienced as possible?

Why not being able to close and move away, perhaps amidst a thousand disturbances, but with the awareness of an end that was inevitable for the respect of both?

Why stay in place, immobile... often indifferent to insults and outrages... amplifying one's pain out of all proportion in a sort of sacrificial delirium whose horror is matched only by its uselessness?

And - above all - why does this state of affairs never seem to end? Do not be limited within a reasonable time frame within which to assess actual opportunities for change...

A superficial observation could lead us to believe the phenomenon due to the lesser ability of modern men and women to bear any kind of frustration, and therefore to establish bonds of dependence simply not being able to accept self-rejection.

But this is not the case. Indeed ... the opposite could be said: that is, that dependence is established precisely because there is rejection. If it were not there, the supposed love would almost always end in an incredibly short amount of time.

As paradoxical as it may seem, addiction feeds on rejection, self-denial, the pain implicit in difficulties and grows in inverse proportion to their insolvability.

What seduces is the fight.

What chains - to use the words of the Milanese psychiatrist Mara Selvini Palazzoli, that is to say the unjustified, absurd, reckless presumption of succeeding. The presumption of being able sooner or later in life to be loved by those who just don't want to know. Or, according to a series of specific variables, to be able to cure those who cannot or do not want to be treated, to save those who cannot or do not want to be saved.

But again, contrary to what can be considered common sense, this compulsion to the bitter end that pushes emotional and employees to remain in their battles useless, is not determined by a kind of psychic masochism. It is not the pleasure of their own suffering that motivates all these people, but just the opposite: the unconscious hope of stitching an old wound. To heal from an ancient evil.

Why the refusal, the ' neglect, the devaluation itself, the humiliation, have already been part of their emotional life; in one way or another these were the crucial experiences that characterized the delicate formative period of their personality. What has been marked!

In an age when emotional autonomy and full consciousness could not yet have formed there have been excruciating experiences of rejection and abandonment by one or both parents, as a result of which children have grown into a sort of anesthesia that hides, however, both the pain-anger ambivalence for the lack of recognition of love, and the atrocious doubt of not being worth much and having to do everything to be better.

The growth covers the wound ... but leaves it insane.

Then, when, in adult life, a situation symbolically similar to that previously experienced arises, it is as if the opportunity to ritualize it was seized on the fly to try to heal the past through the present. The intent of the unconscious is neither foolish nor self-destructive. Rather, he is naive in his presumption of being able to demonstrate once and for all his own affective availability and his own worth, to conquer (cure or heal) being so loved but never conquered, and thus to be compensated for all the missed love.

The Other is almost never seen for what it is (often an egoist withdrawn into himself, or a hopeless neurotic or an unscrupulous profiteer); rather he is imagined as he would be if he finally let himself be loved and lovingly reciprocated so much dedication. It is this image, evoked as for enchantment in unconscious magic mirror that the employee is in love;

without noticing in the least that behind this masking the face of the parent who betrayed him peeks.

The further and final paradox consists in the fact that the symbolic ritual is perceived all the more significant - and therefore all the more coercive - the more the other is emotionally unavailable and not completely conquerable, just as it has never been achieved and never conquered. the abandoned adult . It is no coincidence that the majority of affective-addicts spontaneously confess that they have almost never felt attraction towards others who, despite having all the requisites to be desirable, have made the mistake of bearing witness to a gratuitous affection towards them. As if gratuitousness, in fact, had the power to stifle their desire, which is instead perceived and recognized only in the morbidity of difficulty and rejection. In essence, more than a cognitive and emotional immaturity of the employee, it is a pathological distortion of his emotional life, traced on the distorted imprint impressed by the primary relational model.

Notwithstanding that in any relationship there can be brief painful moments of lack of understanding and incompatibility, the essence of love should consist in the pleasure and joy of sharing the mystery of one's life with another human being. Affective dependence, on the other hand, is characterized by a tension of misunderstandings and hostility, perhaps unconscious but constant, and by the stagnation of the soul in conditions that are as painful and difficult ... under penalty of ending the enchantment and the search for a new relationship even more painful and hopeless, in an almost infinite compulsion to repeat.

CODEPENDENT PERSONALITY

Affective dependence, also known as emotional dependence or codependency (in particular codependency turns out to be a more specific model of emotional dependence, in which the person who suffers from it is oriented towards partners suffering from a serious addiction to substances, or markedly narcissistic partners) can be considered to all intents and purposes as a particular category of dependent personality disorder, in which what determines the addiction is specifically the couple relationship: the essential factor underlying this disorder is constituted by the more or less unconscious attempt of the person who suffers from filling the intrapsychic void experienced and low self-esteem. This type of disorder is also strongly connected to a strong deficit in the ability to manage and modulate emotions and in the ability to establish significant emotional bonds with other people, due to an underlying pattern of markedly insecure attachment (generally of the "anxious- worried "or" anxious-fearful "). Being a type of personality disorder, like all other categories of personality disorder, this also tends to maintain a relatively stable and chronic structure for the entire life span of the person, unless it is appropriately treated with an adequate intervention. Psychotherapeutic. This disorder has various symptoms, which make diagnostic evaluation rather difficult: it can be accompanied by a reactive depression, an obsessive disorder, or even an adjustment disorder, or an anxiety disorder. In emotional dependence, the dynamism of the personality is largely governed by the deep need for the partner and the intense fear of loss and loneliness, which generally end up making the emotional bond established in the couple's relationship extremely difficult and problematic.

According to a study carried out in Spain by the "Espiral Institute Foundation", this disorder would have an incidence of about 10% in the adult population, of which about 75% would be women.

In love relationships, people with emotional dependence show an "anxious" type of attachment to their partner , and are fundamentally characterized by: a continuous and pervasive need to know that they are loved by their partner and the need for constant confirmation; from considerable difficulties in leading an independent life; by the incessant search for a potential partner for an emotional relationship (when they are not in a relationship they are generally pervaded by anxiety), and by a generally hasty choice of the same; from a deep fear of not being loved; from intense fears of losing the object of one's love and frequent jealousies; from contradicting ideas about love and one's feelings; from great difficulty in breaking up the relationship even when it is highly problematic and generates discomfort for the dependent person himself.

GENERAL CHARACTERISTICS OF THE PERSONALITY WITH EMOTIONAL DEPENDENCE

- Strong need to be with the partner, intolerance of loneliness.

- Low self-esteem, which in turn causes a constant need for approval from others, as well as a great fear of rejection and social exclusion.

- Considerable difficulty in saying "no": the wishes and needs of others are continually placed before one's own.

- The emotional addict generally occupies a lower position (one down) in the couple relationship, although this does not exclude the possibility of the opposite, since there is also the " dominant affective dependence ", in which the dependent personality can clearly assume a superior position " one-up", or a position that is only apparently"one down", which in any case allows you to control the ratio.

- Unresolved feelings of guilt, anger, resentment, isolation and fear. All these feelings come from the addicted person's childhood, and from the relationships that were established with the main caregivers.

Thus, usually the couple relationships of people with emotional dependence are frequently very painful, since they usually choose partners who seem paradoxically unable to love them, often people with a high degree of selfishness, egocentrism and narcissism: all this obviously constitutes a great paradox, since the personality with emotional dependence seeks, above all, to be loved. But the paradox is often produced by an improper choice of the type of partner, whose determination is strongly conditioned by internal operating models, by unconscious mental schemes and by a scarce differentiation of the self, whose etiology refers to the models and relational dynamics that characterized the early stages of the evolutionary cycle.

For this reason, the treatment of emotional dependence generally requires a sufficiently long and intensive psychotherapy, which carries out an analytical work of the depth and jointly a work of a cognitive-behavioral type: it is essential to re-elaborate the attributions of meaning of infantile relational dynamics and to restructure mental schemes. Maladjusted and erroneous attitudes that have slowly formed over the course of the various evolutionary phases, resulting in dependent personality traits and a lack of self-esteem.

An emotional dependence not treated adequately involves the high risk that the person who suffers from it remains entangled in one, or in a succession of deleterious emotional relationships, the course of which is strongly counterproductive and extremely painful for one's mental and psychophysical balance.

In broader and more generic terms, codependency indicates the pathological condition in which an individual depends on the pervasive need to be controlled or to control another person (usually the partner). Often this condition involves the lack of consideration of one's own needs, to which a very low priority is systematically granted, instead being excessively concerned with the needs of others, to whom a great importance is attributed. The codependency can occur in any type of relationship, family, work, friendship, torque, and can be characterized by patterns and mechanisms of denial, control, from low self-esteem and excessive accommodation (more rarely also from schemes avoidance). People with narcissistic personality disorder, or with markedly narcissistic traits, are powerful magnets for codependent people.

In general, codependency consists of a constellation of behaviors, thoughts and feelings that go beyond the normal level of self - sacrifice or care. For example, parenting involves taking on roles that require a certain degree of self - sacrifice and giving high priority to the needs of the children, and yet a parent cannot be considered codependent towards the children, unless his / her nurturing function and the degree of parental sacrifice does not reach unhealthy and self-destructive levels. A discriminating aspect with respect to the nature of children's needs is represented by the fact that, while childhood emotional and addictive needs are necessary but temporary, the needs of the codependent person are constant and pervasive.

Often codependent people take on the role of martyrs, and constantly place the needs of others before their own: in doing so they frequently forget to take care of themselves. This, however, gives codependent people the satisfaction of the underlying pervasive need to be "needed," allaying the deep fear of being alone and the intense fear that no one needs them. Codependent people are also constantly looking for acceptance and approval. When it comes to arguing something, they generally tend to take the position of victims, and when they claim something for themselves, they usually feel guilty. The other side of codependency, that is the exact opposite problem, is " counter-dependence ": from the point of view of the "attachment theory" or even of "object relations", we could say that for a counter-dependent person (therefore compulsively self-centered and self-sufficient, compulsively self-referential) the attainment of a healthy level of dependence on some object source outside the Self, can certainly be considered personal progress or psychotherapeutic success. But to return to codependency , below are listed the schemes and the fundamental characteristics that can also constitute self-assessment parameters: in these schemes a series of unconscious defense mechanisms are involved, characteristic of the personality structure of the codependent , and having the purpose avoiding or managing intense and threatening feelings, and / or maintaining self-esteem.

Negation schemes:

- I have a hard time identifying what I feel.

- I minimize, alter or deny how I really feel.

- Compliance schemes:

- I am willing / a sacrifice my values and my integrity in order to avoid rejection and anger of others.

- I am extremely supportive, and I stay in harmful situations for too long.

- I value the opinions and feelings of others more than my own, and I am afraid to personally express and support opinions and feelings that differ from those of others.

- I put my interests and hobbies aside for the purpose of doing what others want.

- I accept sex or sexual attention when I really want affection.

- I make decisions without considering the consequences.

- I give up my positions to gain approval from others or to avoid change.

- Low self-esteem patterns:

- I have a hard time making decisions.

- I harshly judge everything I think, say or do, never considering it "good enough".

- I feel embarrassed / a receive praise, recognition or gifts.

- I don't ask others to fulfill my needs and desires.

- I consider other people's approval of what I think and feel, and how I behave, above my own.

- I don't perceive myself as a lovable and deserving person.

- I am constantly seeking the recognition that I think I deserve.

- I am jealous of the relationships of the people I love, wanting to have them all for myself.

- I have a hard time admitting that I was wrong.

- I need to give a good impression to others, and are even willing / a lie to this.

- I perceive myself as inferior to others.

- I expect others to give me a sense of security.

- I have a hard time getting things started, meeting deadlines and completing projects.

- I have a hard time setting healthy priorities.

- Control schemes:

- I believe that others, for the most part, are unable to take care of themselves.

- I try to convince others of what they "should" think and what they should "really" feel.

- I feel resentful when others do not allow me to help them.

- I freely offer advice and direction to others, without being asked.

- Gifts and favors to those who keep it.

- I use sex to gain approval and acceptance.

- And 'necessary that others have "need" to me if I have a relationship.

- I expect others to meet my needs.

- I decrease my ability to have healthy relationships by avoiding the use of all the tools that could allow me to recover.

- I suppress my feelings and needs to avoid feeling vulnerable.

- I attract others to me, but when they approach I push them away.

- I believe that showing your emotions is a sign of weakness.

- I hold back my expressions of appreciation.

In addition, people who have developed a codependent personality are more likely to attract further abuse from aggressive people into their lives, become entangled in highly stressful jobs or relationships, are more prone to not seek medical help when needed. And less oriented towards the pursuit of important goals and promotions. For some codependents, the social insecurity caused by codependency itself could result in a real anxiety disorder, such as a social phobia, or generalized anxiety disorder, or even an avoidant personality disorder, or a severe syndrome. Depressive, or in a pathological and painful shyness.

As in the case of emotional dependence, codependency , however constituting its own specific type, requires a sufficiently long and intensive psychotherapeutic intervention, thanks to which it is possible to work psycho dynamically on conflicts, immature defense mechanisms, erroneous attitudes, internal operating models of the insecure attachment, and at the same time cognitive work can be conducted on maladaptive mental schemes that support dependent and masochistic personality traits . Often, very marked nuclei of obsessive and histrionic personality are also associated with affective dependence and codependency, as well as the dependent and masochistic ones that generally constitute its supporting axis.

THE SIGNS OF CODEPENDENCY

What are the hallmarks of a codependent personality?

A codependent person has few interests outside the neither relationship nor sources of authentic gratification outside of it: self-satisfaction and validation derive mainly from the ability to satisfy the partner's needs.

The free expression of personal needs is often accompanied by feelings of inadequacy or guilt, to the point of finding it difficult to identify and recognize one's feelings and emotions.

A codependent personality often remains in a relationship even if the partner harms it with his behaviors or has attitudes of abuse not only physical but also psychological.

A codependent person makes extreme sacrifices to please their partner, often sacrificing their time, energy, and well-being.

Codependent people can go so far as to set aside values and principles to satisfy the needs of the partner, who not only accepts and validates this behavior but sometimes even demands it.

A codependent person has the constant and nagging concern of satisfying their partner. This need can induce extreme caution to avoid issues or arguments that may upset the partner or arouse his disappointment. Obviously, the codependent person lives in a continuous state of anxiety in which he carefully evaluates and ponders all his choices to keep the relationship going.

In the past history of a codependent person there are often experiences of addiction, abuse, mental disorders or family trauma. The codependency is a mode adaptive that the person learns to cope psychologically, deny or soothe the pain related to these painful events of the past. How a codependent relationship is born and develops at birth, our survival depends on the parents who provide us with food and give us security and emotional regulation. For a child, the emotional bond that is established with the parents is crucial for both his physical and emotional survival. This first bond of attachment makes the child completely dependent on the parents for the satisfaction of their needs. When a child grows up with an unreliable and available parent, it can happen that the roles are reversed and that he is responsible for the needs of the adult and his safety: in doing so, the child learns to give precedence

to the needs of the adult who, however little available or reliable, remains the point of reference for his survival.

Once he becomes an adult, that child will tend to replicate the same behavioral pattern even with the people he meets, having internalized behavior patterns that will unknowingly lead him to take charge of the needs of others even to the detriment, if not to the detriment, of his own.

The treatment of codependency syndromes therefore starts by analyzing the times related to childhood and observing how these are linked to current behaviors present in adult relationships. It is necessary to recognize the feelings of loss, pain and anger that during the growth phase are associated with the relationship with the parental figures.

The child adapts to the needs of the family context by adapting to the expectations and requests of the parents. However, this effort brings with it the sacrifice of his needs: the result is a deep anger at the disavowal and denial of these needs, necessary for the early assumption of responsibilities and burdens towards adults.

People who in adulthood live a bond of codependency and wish to free themselves, must learn to consider and nurture those aspects of themselves that have been denied up to now.

WHERE TO START?

Feeding and nurturing needs and desires, developing a more authentic connection with self themselves.

Make yourself more autonomous in terms of self-esteem: don't measure your worth only on the willingness to sacrifice yourself for others, but learn to preserve yourself and provide for your well-being, choosing healthier and less dangerous relationships.

Distance yourself from people who have abusive or bullying behavior. Relationships are no longer based on a unilateral bond of exclusive availability to the requests of the other but on a criterion of reciprocity and greater equity in exchanges.

Establish clearer boundaries between one and others, avoiding situations of fusion in which the needs of the other become predominant over one's own. It is often a long and tiring path that brings with it the need to face a change, giving up addictive modalities which, although dysfunctional, guaranteed a form of security and stability with respect to the role of constant support and help.

Often the idea of being indispensable seems to be the key to keeping the other tied to oneself, by virtue not so much of a free and authentic choice, but rather of the advantages that the possibility of having such a helpful person brings to one's side. Acquiring the awareness that everyone is responsible for their own personal fulfillment means understanding that individual value is not measured with acts of extreme sacrifice, but with the possibility and the ability to make choices that safeguard the other but also oneself.

In a healthy relationship, both partners depend on each other for love, emotional support, and encouragement.

A codependent relationship, on the other hand, is one-sided. It is a dysfunctional dynamic in which a partner gives himself disproportionately, sacrificing his own needs and desires to please - and repair the damage - the other, who instead often ends up behaving recklessly, and only on his part, he rarely offers his support to the other.

"On the one hand there are those who manifest their love mostly through an offer of help, on the other hand there are those who feel loved mainly when they receive help", he adds. "The intensity of sharing the other's difficulties, troubles and assistance provided deepen the emotional bond and that feeling of intimacy".

Some alarm bells.

1. Say "yes" to your partner quickly, without stopping to think about how you feel.

"Within a relationship you are entitled to take care of yourself, setting limits - seeking inner strength to say 'no' or 'not sure', where there is something you do not see ' it belongs, or have need more time to consider the partner's request. "

2. Often try to make excuses for - or remedying - your partner's behaviors.

"For example, glossing over the fact that he drinks, or making excuses to justify it in the eyes of friends, is likely a sign that you are not objective in your relationship, because those limits are blurred."

3. Partner happiness becomes number one priority.

"Such a relationship is truly toxic to individual development, and ultimately to one's happiness. And yet, unaware of the repercussions of such misplaced devotion, the codependent cannot help but continue to try to please the person he is. supporting, because that appreciation was given the highest, sometimes the only, priority ".

4. By getting your partner out of trouble for the umpteenth time you are convinced you are helping him. But now all you do is go along with it.

"In your eyes you show love by indulging and saving your partner, and you do it by helping him to solve his own self-

produced problems. This means that your loving gestures of support go to fuel a sick addiction, physical or mental health problems, irresponsibility, immaturity, addictions or criminal behavior ".

5. You lose sense of your identity, your interests and desires.

"Healthy love leaves room for differences. Each of you will have their own sense of self while remaining emotionally connected in the event of a disagreement or clash. Differences within the relationship are not taken personally. Each will have their own friends, their own interests, each will support the other, and their happiness does not depend on the relationship. There is an individual sense of self and a sense of 'being together'.

Codependent love exists when each partner ends up giving up a part of the person they are, in the name of safeguarding the relationship. The dynamic is based on manipulation, control, the blurring of borders and the renunciation of certain aspects of oneself ".

6. The partner plays dirty and often manipulates you to win .

"A healthy love affair includes clear boundaries in communication, even in the event of conflict. Healthy couples resolve disputes quickly; they do not block, harbor a grudge or manipulate their partners."

7. Always give your partner more than you get in return.

"Codependents give their partner far more than they get in return. While they do it to ' secure' attachment - thereby containing rejection anxiety - in the process they neglect their own legitimate relational wants and needs."

8. The partner regularly exploits your qualities.

"You find yourself in a relationship with someone who uses your love and your empathic and collaborative nature to escape their responsibilities as adults and / or not to take charge of their own life and the consequences of their irresponsibility, immaturity, addictions , physical or mental health problems or criminal behavior ".

9. Try to take on your partner's pain and difficulties.

"Codependents come to feel deeply uncomfortable at the idea of leaving the other to their pain. Metaphorically, we take it upon ourselves and carry it upon us. Unfortunately we end up mostly paying for it ourselves, and we can end up with it. Feel intense resentment, giving up some aspects of our person. We become convinced that we are responsible for the feelings of the other and / or the fact that our happiness depends on our permanence in the relationship."

10. Your relationship is based on behavior designed to condition, control and constrain.

"For example, ' If you really loved me you wouldn't make me angry enough to feel the need to ease the tension with alcohol.' Or, ' When we get married, you'll have to stop dating.'"

CODEPENDENCY AND ANXIETY

Suffering from panic attacks, phobias and other anxiety spectrum disorders, refers to unresolved emotional and psychological dynamics, regarding the process of separation, evolution and personal growth.

Usually, in fact, the first crises emerge in conjunction with "big steps in life" (university, marriage, change of job, marital crisis) or important bereavement: in both cases the person is called to an enormous personal effort to acquire independence necessary to walk on one's own legs, to give life a very specific direction.

The motivation is linked to the difficulty of managing conflict, separation and often the inability to create new structures that replace old schemes. In fact, it would be a necessary evolution to "reinvent oneself", but in this case the person cannot manage the anguish of loss, abandonment and guilt.

Those who suffer from anxiety disorders are afraid of losing (through their own fault or inadequacy) people and affections considered fundamental for them and for this reason they "avoid" any type of conflict and sabotage any attempt at emancipation with "anxiety attacks " . Which thus put everything back in place, protecting the individual in his role as victim-dependent.

Very often in fact, it happens to be faced with people who in the grip of anxiety crises stop driving for fear of being alone in the car and having no one to help them in the event of a panic attack.

If we think about it for a moment, the car is the symbol of autonomy par excellence, but not only. The car symbolizes one's life, and it is unthinkable for the anxious-addicted person to take on such a responsibility.

At the base there is in fact a deep sense of inadequacy and vulnerability summarized in the phrases "I'm not worth enough" and "something terrible could happen", combined with a pattern of dependence: "I can't do it alone"

Anxious people have been anxious children (defined by Ainsworth as "resistant"), who have not been able to use their mother or caregiver as a safe base to explore the world. Our "internal operating model" of relationship with the mother unfolds in childhood in the relationship with brothers and friends, in adolescence it is applied to the first "emotional relationship", and then becomes more rooted and evident in the stable relationship of marriage or coexistence.

Anxious adults constantly fear rejection and abandonment discourage the autonomy and independence of those they love, using their own difficulties as an alibi to prevent them from drifting away. The triggered mechanism refers to one's potential and basic beliefs which are then confirmed with action. Let's see better: if I am convinced that I am not worth it and that if something negative happens alone I will not succeed, I ignore my potential or underestimate it, I take actions that prevent me from experiencing my effectiveness and consequently the results I will get will be in line with my basic beliefs: that alone I can't do it and I need someone next to me to guide and support me in things.

Ultimately, anxiety, addiction and passive behavioral style often go hand in hand starting from the same basis: an insecure attachment that determines relationships based on submission, fear of abandonment and an adhesive emotionality, in which the other is what he knows. What is best for us, which protects us from the dangerous world but at the same time can be hyper-present and suffocate us by controlling us.

The double-edged sword of this relational modality is precisely this: the other controls and suffocates us, while we continue to delegate our existence and the responsibility for leading it to him.

Hence the conflict that discourages any attempt at autonomy often also implemented on the other hand: ultimately, if on the one hand the anxious and dependent person requires presence-support, on the other hand those who are on the other side feel the weight. Of responsibility, but at the same time has the advantage of being able to control the person as well as obtaining the narcissistic return linked to one's own importance?

Let's take an example.

A woman is convinced that she is not intelligent enough to take care of the chores related to the economic administration of the house: she leaves her husband who relieves her of these responsibilities, controls the economic performance of the house, centers the economic power, while she experiences frustration for not being able, for needing her husband in these things, but, never taking the initiative, nourishes her own conviction of not being up to it, perhaps even feeling anger towards herself for this, and towards the husband "more capable ".

It is therefore often an unhealthy mechanism that ensures that for each anxious-dependent-victim subject, there is the other guide-control-executioner.

This is why it is important to work on the patterns that feed addiction and the sense of vulnerability connected to anxious symptoms: experiencing and building oneself as incapable, inadequate leads the individual to focus his selective attention on what are his own defects, shortcomings and any write-downs in the case of tasks that require the use of skills and potential that he is the first to recognize. Hence the appearance of symptoms of anxiety that allow it to delegate to others and thus avoid (the avoidance is the best form of reinforcement of dysfunctional behaviors) to experiment instead as a person capable.

Dependence allows you to feel protected and safe, while the other is satisfied because he controls and feels important. In reality, when this mechanism crosses the threshold of the credible by completely moving away from reality, it becomes deleterious for oneself and counterproductive for the relationship: that is no longer love, it is submission.

Confusing love and the need for protection and support is deleterious in a relationship: if you don't develop an autonomous personality, a physical and emotional independence that gives us a solid identity as individuals, you can end up getting caught up in unhappy relationships, from which you do not even have the courage to leave because loneliness is too frightening.

Building and experimenting ourselves every day, learning from experiences without judging ourselves incapable, but as human beings who "collect life experiences", allows us to face the various daily situations as opportunities for growth and not as a test bed to measure our worth.

Making mistakes is human, learning is important, but staying locked in a relationship that acts as an alibi is the greatest damage we can do, because we are condemning ourselves to immobility by delegating someone else to live our life.

Let us remember that every day can be the first of a new life where we can be protagonists without the need for stunts anymore.

AFFECTIVE DEPENDENCE, ANXIOUS TRAITS AND ATTACHMENT STYLE

Affective Addiction is a clinical category that has emerged in recent years, investigating it through research is useful for setting up an effective psychotherapy

Affective Addiction (or Love Addiction) can be framed in the general field of "new addictions", a class of heterogeneous disorders (such as addiction to gambling, work, the internet) characterized by a strong involvement in repetitive and persistent behaviors , which significantly compromise the person's relational, social and professional life . As attachment studies teach us, the need for physical and psychological closeness to another human being is a basic need of the individual.

We talk about Love Addiction when the search for the other is obsessive, characterized by continuous requests for absolute devotion and renunciation on the part of the beloved, social closure and avoidance , total dedication to the wishes of the other and a failure to recognize one's own needs. , needs, desires and even one's own identity.

It is a very often dangerous disorder, as the affective dependent subject tends to get involved in entangling relationships with people who tend to be violent and aggressive towards whom he triggers his own addiction, capable of filling ancient emotional gaps.

The Love Addiction is a little-known disease, which only in recent years has become a topic of interest in scientific research, probably because of the "new addictions" is, in general, a clinical category that has emerged particularly since the last years. In fact, this disorder has not yet found space in an official classification; however it is a phenomenon that is increasingly found in the context of clinical activity (Manfredi, 2016).

Therefore, in order not to find ourselves disoriented and disoriented with respect to those who bring us problems of this kind, it is therefore important to orient the research activity in this direction, in order to better understand emotional dependence and to obtain the necessary tools for effective psychotherapy.

Consequently, we decided to carry out research that would investigate some specificities of this form of psychopathology. In particular, we were interested in deepening the relationship between Love Addiction and state anxiety, as well as between Love Addiction and anxious relational style. In fact , according to the theoretical model suggested by Sassaroli, anxiety would seem to be an important factor in the cognitive functioning of the affective addict: anxiety assumes an important role in maintaining the disorder.

On the basis of the statistical results just reported, the initial hypothesis therefore appears to be confirmed and it is possible to state that state anxiety is significantly correlated to emotional dependence, being indeed the greatest predictor among those measured, with a significant direct effect on the manifestations of this pathology. The power of anxiety as a factor involved in the cognitive functioning of the affective addict is also demonstrated by the existence of a statistically significant correlation between anxious relational style and affective dependence, which suggests the existence of an important mediating effect exerted by the subject's anxious traits. in the development and maintenance of emotional dependence.

What emerged therefore opens up a scenario in which it is possible to explore new and interesting perspectives aimed at guaranteeing a broader spectrum approach to the treatment of emotional dependence.

On the one hand, the framing of anxious factors in the development and maintenance of the pathology allows for a timely treatment of the disorder on the basis of what have proved being the protocols already effective in the management of pathologies connected to the anxious spectrum. The intervention on those that have been identified as the main factors involved in anxiety disorders would allow to interrupt a vicious circle which, within the relational context, often acquires an even greater gravity and great suffering from which, however, the patient struggles to get away due to the strong fear of loneliness, which is perhaps today the greatest fear within our society which, in order to stay away from you, is constantly looking for new means of digital and technological connection. On the other hand, the identification of the more nuclear aspects linked to the image of oneself and to the vision of the Self with Others allows us to arrive at the central node of the pathology and to prepare the conditions for lasting change. Considering that most people who live in a situation of emotional dependence show traits of an anxious type, the goal of therapy should first of all be the creation of a setting capable of offering a sense of security that allows a free exploration of oneself and of the relationship towards achieving the expression of one's true self. Finally, from the point of view of the therapeutic alliance, the identification of these factors could facilitate the clinician in the enhancement of the aspects capable of guaranteeing the creation of a genuine, authentic, non-judgmental and truly helpful relationship for the patient, allowing him to living the experience of an emotionally corrective relationship. In this way it is possible to create the necessary conditions to be able to have access to what is the painful theme, often linked to an experience of unworthiness or non-love, which characterizes people who suffer from emotional dependence.

CODEPENDENT PERSONALITY DISORDER

Although affective dependence, due to insufficient experimental data, is not included among the mental disorders diagnosed in DSM-5, the Diagnostic and Statistical Manual of Mental Disorders (American Psychiatric Association , 2013), it is classified among the "New Addiction ", new behavioral addictions, including Internet addiction, pathological gambling, sex addiction, sports addiction, compulsive shopping, work addiction.

Reynaud's group (Reynaud, Karila, Blecha and Benyamina, 2010), starting from the analogies found with substance addiction, proposes a diagnostic definition of love addiction, based on the duration and frequency of perceived suffering, it presents for the first five criteria):

Existence of a withdrawal syndrome due to the absence of the loved one, characterized by significant suffering and a compulsive need for the other;

Considerable amount of time spent on this relationship (in reality or in thought);

Reduction of important social, professional or leisure activities;

Persistent desire or unsuccessful efforts to reduce or control one's relationship;

Search for the relationship, despite the existence of problems created by it;

Existence of attachment difficulties, as manifested by one of the following:

(a) Repeated exalted love affairs, without any period of lasting attachment;

(b) Repeated painful love affairs, characterized by insecure attachment ".

ROMANTIC LOVE OR EMOTIONAL ADDICTION?

A certain degree of dependence on the partner is part of any love story that can be said to be such, especially in the phase of falling in love, characterized by a strong sense of intimacy and passion, in which the sense of fusion is particularly strong.

Some authors (Fisher, Xu, Aron and Brown, 2016) describe the presence, in individuals in the phase of romantic love, of symptoms characteristic of addictive disorders, including euphoria, desire, tolerance, emotional and physical addictions, withdrawal and relapse.

Romantic love is a natural part of the biological imperative of human reproduction and corresponds to a specific pattern of physiological, psychological and behavioral characteristics, which includes: attention focused on the object of love, reorganization of priorities, an increase in energy and feelings of euphoria, mood swings, sympathetic nervous system responses such as sweating and heartbeat, elevated sexual desire and sexual possessiveness , obsessive thoughts about each other, desire for emotional union gestures, purpose-oriented and intense behavior motivation to obtain and maintain the bond.

When the most dependent characteristics become rigid and pervasive and take on the connotation of absolute necessity, the risk is to fall into the most dysfunctional side of the love bond, that relating to pathological emotional dependence.

The possibility of going beyond the phase of falling in love and loving the other, in fact, depends precisely on the ability of the members of the couple to perceive and respect each other as separate individuals that is to recognize the other in his diversity without losing sight of each other. Your individuality.

On the other hand, when the couple bond obscures one's own needs and desires and chains us to the other, suffocating our individuality, we can speak of love addiction or emotional dependence.

Note that, in English, the term addiction refers to a general condition in which psychological dependence leads to the search for the object of interest, without which life would lose its value. Reynaud and collaborators (Reynaud, Karila, Blecha and Benyamina, 2010), clearly define the differences between love and addiction, meaning with the term Love Passion a universal and necessary state for human beings, which implies a functional attachment to others, and with Love Addiction is a maladaptive condition characterized by an imperious need and desire for the other that translate into problematic relational patterns, characterized by the persistent and assiduous search for closeness, despite the awareness of the negative consequences of such behavior.

The transition to a dysfunctional falling in love would take place through the transformation of desire into necessary need and pleasure into suffering. This would be accompanied by extreme obstinacy in seeking and maintaining the relationship, despite the awareness of the negative consequences. Being compulsive desire (craving), obsessive commitment, perseverance of problematic behaviors and the impairment of the control systems of these, characteristic elements of behavioral addictions, it is possible to assume that love addiction is due to a dysfunctional stiffening of natural characteristics of romantic love.

Affective Dependence and Similarities to Drug Addiction

Falling in love and drug addiction has many similarities; both lovers and drug addicts experience:

Intense euphoria when they see the partner, similar to the euphoria that characterizes the use of a drug

Craving (which is a spasmodic and uncontrollable desire) for the partner or for drugs

Tendency to seek more and more closeness with the partner (phenomenon similar to tolerance, a mechanism that pushes drug addicts to progressively increase the amount of drug usually taken to obtain the desired effect)

When a relationship ends , people in love have withdrawal symptoms that are similar to those found in drug abstinence syndrome (depression, anxiety, insomnia or hypersomnia , irritability, loss of appetite or binge eating) which, just like occurs in drug addiction, lead to relapse; e.g. having a relapse in emotional addiction means looking for a partner again despite being unfaithful, violent, etc.

The similarities between falling in love and drug addiction are also confirmed by neuroimaging studies (which visualize brain activity in vivo). These studies show that the ' falling in love activates certain brain regions which is rich in dopamine (a substance that is released in your brain every time we do something nice like eg. Eat, have sex, look after infants etc.). The pleasure we feel serves to motivate us to repeat these behaviors and therefore to ensure the survival of the individual and the species. As demonstrated by numerous empirical evidence these same regions are activated both in substance dependence that in behavioral addictions such as compulsive shopping.

Exactly as happens in substance addiction, also in Affective Addiction with the passage of time everything inexorably revolves around the partner; often the dependent person withdraws or deliberately avoids others in an attempt to protect themselves from criticism or the feared abandonment.

Usually both interests and hobbies are progressively abandoned and the focus of existence becomes the partner; also the work performance decreases because the person has his mind constantly occupied by his sentimental problems and spends a lot of time brooding to try to solve them.

In extreme cases, eg. Even when your partner is violent physically dependent patients tend to justify it, they isolate, lying or do not ask for help in order to protect it; unfortunately often they are unable to leave it even when their physical safety is at risk. Generally, patients with Affective Addiction are aware of the devastating effects that their partner has on their life, but just like drug addicts, they cannot abstain from the relationship.

INTERPERSONAL CYCLES IN EMOTIONAL DEPENDENCE

Affective Addiction sufferers feel inadequate and unworthy of love and constantly live in fear of being abandoned by their partner. The fear of abandonment leads to the attempt to control the other with complacent behaviors of extreme sacrifice, availability and care, with the hope of making the relationship stable and lasting.

The very tendency to build a relationship of non-mutuality, but in which the other and his needs are central, leads to leave room for self-centered and an affective personalities , which end up confirming in those suffering from emotional dependence the fear of not being able to be worthy of love. in fact , low self-esteem pushes the person suffering from emotional dependence to read the lack of availability of the other not as information about the other ("he is a self-centered narcissus"), but as information about himself ("he doesn't love me because I well").

The result is an increase in sacrifice and a continuous blame for the unsatisfactory performance of the relationship; the other is chased exactly as gamblers do who "chase loss" and can't stop gambling.

Sometimes, due to a wrong suffered by the partner, anger can momentarily push those suffering from Affective Addiction to say enough and to end the relationship, but inevitably, the withdrawal symptoms (depression and inability to experience pleasure, anxiety, feeling of emptiness etc.) push to forgive the partner and justify him, thus returning to the vicious circle of a toxic relationship.

AFFECTIVE ADDICTION AND PERSONALITY DISORDERS

In clinical practice we often encounter patients who are unable to interrupt deeply destructive intimate relationships, which generate suffering and compromise their life on various levels.

Patients with Dependent Personality Disorder are characterized by dependence on others, that is, they are unable to live independently and always need advice and reassurance. When they are alone they feel helpless and without points of reference, they constantly live with the terror of being abandoned by their partner.

In order to avoid the feared abandonment, they are willing to do unpleasant and degrading things (they allow themselves to be exploited economically or sexually, tolerate infidelity and in extreme cases violence). But the Affective dependence is not only the prerogative of the Employee Disorder; even patients with Borderline Personality Disorder have serious difficulties in being alone and adopt dependent behaviors (they put themselves at the complete disposal of their partner and idealize them). They have chaotic emotional relationships characterized by an overwhelming passion but also by violent discussions; patients with this disorder live with the fear of being abandoned by their partner but also fear of depending on him and of losing their autonomy.

Patients with Histrionic Personality Disorder fear loneliness and are overwhelmed by anguish in the face of separation; they constantly need attention, approval and support. Contrary to what one might think, even those suffering from Narcissistic Personality Disorder are not immune from emotional dependence on their partner. The so-called narcissists covert fact are plagued by constant thoughts of failure, show poor self-esteem, are very attentive to the judgments of others, and chew constantly, reports show an anxious attachment due to the constant fear of rejection and abandonment.

Affective dependence and predisposing factors

Stavola and collaborators (Stavola, Mazzocato, Brambilla, Flower, 2015), have carried out a research on the factors predisposing the emotional dependence, on the assumption that it is linked to the presence of phenomena of dissociation and deregulation emotional consequent to a trauma infantile and to the style of insecure attachment . To investigate the correlation between the disorder and the constructs examined, the authors submitted a series of self-report questionnaires to an experimental group of 99 individuals, recruited through GADA (Affective Self Help Dependence Groups), and to a control group of 75 people: the Childhood Trauma Questionnaire - Short Form (Bernstein and Fink , 1998) for trauma, the Relationship Questionnaire (Bartholomew and Horowitz, 1991) for attachment, the Dissociative Experience Scale (Carlson and Putnam , 1993) for dissociation and the Difficulties Emotion Regulation Scale (Gratz and Roemer , 2004) for emotional deregulation . The results made it possible to confirm an model of love addiction which identifies, as predisposing factors, the presence of traumas of emotional abuse and emotional neglect, the styles of preoccupied and fearful attachment, the presence of dissociative symptoms at the pathological level, the difficulty , clinically significant, in the regulation of emotions.

Affective dependence and treatment in psychotherapy

The treatment of emotional dependence is structured on the achievement of short and long-term goals:

The first, short-term goal is to address and resolve the patient's current suffering in terms of symptoms and behavioral dysfunctions.

The second, long-term goal is to address early experiences of abandonment, physical and emotional neglect, mistreatment, abuse, etc. which are generally the basis of the belief that they are worthless and not worthy of being loved that characterize patients who suffer from Affective Addiction. In parallel, the therapy aims to help patients have access to what they feel, their desires and their purposes and to use them to make autonomous choices. In this way, one of the nuclei of dependent personalities is repaired, which is the lack of agency , or rather to carry out an action plan that is born within, even in conditions of lack of relational support or adversity.

Thanks to this work, the foundations are created so that patients can on the one hand form emotional relationships based on reciprocity in which they finally feel loved and accepted, or so that they can maintain a sense of amiability and personal value, accompanied by a sense of activity even when such relationships are missing.

CODEPENDENT BEHAVIORS

The codependency (or codependency) is a dynamic for which a person is influenced in an excessive and therefore pathological behavior of another person who is seeking at the same time to control or correct. The other person can be any significant subject in the codependent's life: a partner, a parent, a child, a friend. This is usually suffering from some form of addiction, such as substances (drugs or alcohol), but not only (gambling, compulsive shopping, sex compulsive). Anyone who bonds with an alcoholic or drug addict is animated by the hope of saving him, of healing him from addiction. He dedicates his life to the recovery of the other, fight. He endures humiliations, sacrifices, economic deficits, sometimes real to his own physical violence. Yet he remains trapped in the relationship, he clings to it, does not give up. The partner has an addiction to alcohol, substance. The codependent has a dependency on the partner. Or, even more irrationally, an addiction to wanting to save him from the enemy and rival: alcohol, another drug addiction or compulsive practice.

The concept of codependency arises in the field of drug addiction and alcoholism. In fact, many partners of alcoholics and drug addicts tend both to repeat past scripts (choice of partners with the same addiction that a previous partner or parent suffered) and to put the well-being and "salvation" of the other at the center of their lives. .

Depending on the clinical approach adopted and the case considered, codependency can be defined as an isolated dynamic (i.e. which occurs only once in a lifetime, towards a single subject), a predisposition, a personality or character trait, a real psychological, chronic and progressive disorder. In the latter case, codependents need to relate to dependent people for an insane form of well-being. The choice of an alcoholic or drug addict partner who needs a "savior" or the codependent.

The characteristics of the codependent subjects can be summarized as follows:

- They focus their lives on others

- To their life it depends on others

- They seek happiness outside of themselves

- They help others instead of themselves

- They desire the esteem and love of others

- They control the behavior of others

- They try to catch others in error

- They anticipate the needs of others

- They are attracted to people in need of help

- They attribute their malaise to others

- They feel responsible for the behavior of others

- They increasingly tolerate other people's behaviors that they would not have previously endured

- They experience symptoms of anxiety and depression

- They have an obsessive fear of losing each other

- They develop feelings of guilt for the wrong behaviors of the other

- They often come from families with experiences of codependency

From the list of these characteristics, many points in common with affective and relational addictions emerge. The difference of the bottom is in emotional dependencies there is not always a troublesome partner like in codependency.

Some forms of codependency can also develop in cases where one or both partners seek compensation for their deficiencies, their unmet needs, in order to support each other. For example, those who are more instinctive look for people who have developed the rational aspect more and vice versa. In this case a dysfunctional relationship develops, since it is not a form of complementarities, but a symbiotic relationship.

Frequently, when one of the two decides to "evolve", or rather implements behaviors that allow him to begin to overcome his need for dependence on his partner, the other inevitably feels betrayed and abandoned, as he feels the loss of that relationship that made him feel safe. In fact, this type of dysfunctional relationship, like all symbiotic relationships, does not involve changes, but equilibrium, staticity, dependence.

To overcome this dysfunctional relationship, it is first of all necessary to recognize the existence of the dynamics that cause dysfunctional behaviors and then to begin a process of changing one's way of relating to others.

Affective addiction is part of the "new addictions ", that is, processes that have the same characteristics as drug addiction, but are not caused by the action of an abusive substance. At the present time , emotional dependence is not considered as a diagnosis but, starting from the 1970s, it has been explored and defined, to an increasing extent, as an autonomous disorder, which presents aspects common to all types of addiction and, at the at the same time, peculiar characteristics that concern falling in love and the sentimental relationship.

All forms of addiction have something in common: they can be seen as attempts to keep one's emotions in check through experiences that serve the following functions:

- Relieve boredom

- Increase feelings of well-being

- Remove sadness, pain and any kind of unpleasant emotion

What, on the other hand, differentiates one addiction from another, is precisely the particular experience, or behavior, which helps the person to manage the ups and downs of his life and which, with the establishment of addiction, becomes an inevitable trap. In the case of substance addiction, for example, the experience in question is represented by the use of drugs, and the function of escape from reality and pain that they cover.

In the case of emotional dependence, experiences fall into two categories:

Romantic fantasies, which help to lessen the fear of loneliness and rejection, promising "eternal happiness"

The experience of the bond of attachment, which calms the fear, conscious or unconscious, of being abandoned and the illusion of eliminating loneliness and deficiencies in self- esteem

For some people, relationships become a source of dissatisfaction and frustration, but as difficult as carrying on this bond seems, the thought of being without it is far worse. Affective dependence is established precisely within this tension between "not being able to live with" and "not being able to live without": the functioning of the person depends on one's own emotional relationship.

In the early stages of falling in love, people exhibit various addiction-related symptoms, both substance and behavioral, including euphoria, withdrawal, tolerance, physical and psychological dependence, relapse. Love, therefore, could be compared to a substance of abuse, and from both it is possible to develop an addiction. The emotional responses, in both cases, are closely linked to physical reactions, creating a powerful push towards establishing or maintaining an emotional relationship: the relationship, therefore, becomes the goal and, at the same time, the reward. , which will allow the addicted person to reduce suffering and feel better.

One of the brain centers linked to reward is located within the limbic system: this area constitutes the control center of emotional responses, governing the release of dopamine, a neurotransmitter that induces feelings of well-being and euphoria. Some substances, such as cocaine for example, stimulate an increase in the release (or a decrease in reabsorption) of dopamine. Behavioral addictions can also create conditions in which dopamine production is stimulated: the brain, in this case, is "trained" to release dopamine in correspondence with particular behaviors, such as shopping or gambling or, in this case, chance, and closeness to the person - object of the addiction.

It could be said that love seems to be a kind of natural addiction, a "normal psychophysical alteration" experienced by most human beings at least once in their life. The romantic relationship, therefore, could be a "positive" addiction, when the relationship is mutual and non-toxic, but easily become a dangerously negative addiction when it is inappropriate, not reciprocal or not reciprocated.

The signs and symptoms of emotional addiction are, in large part, mirror image of those of behavioral addictions, and include:

The pleasure deriving from the object of addiction

Tolerance: the constant need to increase the time spent with the partner while decreasing the time invested in independent activities or contacts with other people

Withdrawal: the appearance of very intense negative emotions, such as anxiety, panic, depression, when the partner is physically or emotionally distant

Loss of control: the inability to reflect clearly on one's situation and to control one's behavior, alternating with moments of lucidity in which the dependent person experiences shame and remorse

In daily life, these signs and symptoms are reflected in a wide variety of emotional employee behaviors and attitudes:

Your partner's emotions are more important than your own

Self-esteem depends on the approval of the other

Taking a position or a decision becomes difficult and causes strong feelings of guilt

The fear of being abandoned is so intense that most behaviors have the function of avoiding loneliness and rejection

Recognizing and expressing one's thoughts and emotions is difficult or scary

Most of your time is spent on controlling your partner

The negative consequences that the relationship produces in all other areas are ignored

The characteristics of an emotional dependence, however, are largely intertwined with the traits of an addictive personality: in fact, people who find themselves addicted to a relationship often have the following personality traits:

Difficulty in making decisions, even daily ones, without asking for advice and reassurance. The lack of confidence in their ability to make correct choices, and extreme guilt when you make mistakes makes the terrifying possibility of mistakes

Need for other people to take responsibility for important areas of their life. Daily challenges become insurmountable difficulties and impossible to face alone

Difficulty disagreeing with others. An addicted person feels that they are not valuable enough to express a personal opinion that differs from that of someone on whom they depend

Difficulty completing projects or activities independently. The fear, in this case, is that other people may notice failure, perceived as inevitable

Negative emotions such as anxiety or despair at the thought of being alone or being able to be alone

Taking the blame or responsibility for negative events or situations, even when it is not true or when it is not possible to identify a responsible person. Blame yourself is a way of maintaining control over circumstances that are very often uncontrollable

Inability to create or defend their own spaces or borders.

THE TYPES OF EMOTIONAL EMPLOYEES

The American Association Employees anonymous affective (Love Addicted Anonymous) has outlined some typical profiles of emotional employees:

Obsessive affective addict. He cannot detach himself from his relationship, even if the partner is not emotionally or sexually available, unable to communicate, distant, devaluing, abusive, self-centered, selfish, controlling, in turn dependent on something else (alcohol, drugs, gambling).

Co- dependent affective employee. In most cases, he suffers from a lack of self-esteem and tries, by all means, to keep the person he depends on with him, for example by taking care of him, controlling him with passive - aggressive strategies, or accepting abuse. Typically, the codependent emotional addict would do anything to "take care" of their partner, in the hope that someday they will be reciprocated.

Dependent on the relationship. Unlike the other types, he is no longer in love with his partner, but still fails to leave him. Usually, they are extremely unhappy and afraid of change and the possibility of being alone.

Narcissistic affective addict. This type of employee uses seduction and domination to control their partner. Unlike the codependent, who accepts suffering, the narcissist does not let something interfere with his well-being and does not appear to be concerned about the relationship in any way. When, however, he is faced with the threat of abandonment, he tries by all means to maintain the relationship, up to the point of violence.

Ambivalent affective employee. This category generally suffers from avoidant personality disorder, which causes an exhausting search for love, but at the same time the terror of intimacy. This combination can lead, in some cases, to seeking the love of unavailable people while, in others, to breaking off relationships as they begin to become more intimate and serious.

Refusing seducer. This emotional addict searches for a partner to get affection, companionship or sex and then, when he feels insecure, reject him, in a continuous cycle of availability and unavailability.

Romantic employee. The addiction, in this case, involves multiple partners. In contrast to sexual addicts, who try to avoid bonding, romantic addicts form bonds with all of their partners, to varying degrees, even if relationships are short-lived or develop simultaneously.

COGNITIVE - BEHAVIORAL THERAPY FOR AFFECTIVE ADDICTION

As with other kinds of addiction, healing from emotional addiction is a complex process that, in some cases, can take some time. The fundamental presuppositions, in any case, are the recognition of one's addiction, the awareness of the consequences it has produced and could produce in the future and the willingness to undertake a process of change. All of this requires an initial dose of courage because, in most cases, it involves ending the dysfunctional relationship and starting to manage abstinence.

Cognitive -behavioral therapy for affective addiction consists of several stages and begins with the assessment and formulation of the case. Specifically, therapist and patient retrace the history of the current and past relationship, outlining the events that contributed to the establishment of the basic beliefs of unloveliness and, ultimately, of emotional dependence as a way to fill and compensate these cores. In the same phase, short, medium and long-term goals are jointly set and a support network is set up for the patient, identifying some trusted people to be involved who can help him, especially in the early stages of abstinence.

Awareness of the disorder, of its dynamics and of the vicious circles that are established represents the step immediately following the conceptualization of the case: the recognition of the mechanisms of addiction by the patient becomes fundamental to understand how to manage any relapses.

The work with cognitive - behavioral therapy focuses, in this case, mainly on the restructuring of dysfunctional beliefs linked to one's own value and amiability and on the management of emotions linked to the fear of loneliness, rejection and abandonment. In this phase of the journey, the therapist also helps the patient to modify the unrealistic expectations of love.

One component of cognitive-behavioral therapy for affective addiction is assertiveness training. The ability to recognize and express one's needs and emotions, in fact, contributes to the construction of a more solid sense of self and of one's autonomy, while maintaining a constant relational connection with the other.

From a behavioral point of view, the therapy includes direct interventions aimed at helping the patient to interrupt old patterns of action, such as, for example, entering into new relationships before having recognized their needs or established personal boundaries, or ignoring some alarming signals . in the abusive behavior of the partner, or put their own needs in the background.

When the therapeutic relationship appears consolidated, in a more advanced stage of therapy, the work focuses on a complex yet crucial area in emotional dependence: the acceptance and management of painful emotions. Feelings such as guilt, remorse or shame, for a long time denied and hidden during the dysfunctional relationship of addiction, are brought out within the protected setting of the session and, gradually, accepted as an integral part of one's person, in the here. and now.

In some cases, cognitive - behavioral therapy can be integrated with Mindfulness techniques , which are very useful for managing rumination on one's relationship, current or past, while promoting, at the same time, openness and awareness of one's emotions and an attitude compassionate towards oneself.

CODEPENDENCY AND FAMILY

The codependency, a psychological condition or a relationship in which a person is controlled or manipulated by another suffering from a pathological condition, tends to reproduce once the "victims" are in turn to have a family. Parents who experienced this reality as children can break the vicious circle of codependency by exploring and acquiring different styles of parenting.

In fact, there are several strategies that can help in this and that are also useful for those who are not parents, to "re-educate themselves" and remedy what they did not have in childhood by their parents - unconditional love, the possibility of expressing their own feelings or respect.

THE CHILDHOOD TRAUMA HAVE LONG-LASTING EFFECTS

Many people who have suffered trauma during their childhood continue to feel the effects of these wrongs even in adulthood.

To cope with the trauma, traits of codependency may have been developed, such as trying to solve other people's problems or "saving" others, behaving like a martyr, a tendency to perfectionism, overwork, a tendency to feel in control, the difficulty in trusting, denying oneself, feeling guilty and ashamed, the difficulty of identifying and expressing one's feelings, being overly compliant, angry, blaming, indignant, self-critical and self-deprecating.

The codependent is "transmitting" within families

If you have codependent traits, there is a good chance that your parents and grandparents also did. The codependency involuntarily "passes" from one generation to another. Parents and those who care for a child are his or her first teachers; therefore they have a huge influence on the development of his self-control and conception of his personal worth (how he thinks about himself and how he treats himself).

As codependency is "learned," parents unwittingly shape and teach their children codependent ways of thinking and acting.

For example: Maria was emotionally abused by her parents and grew up feeling out of love and shame, without the coping skills needed to manage her feelings. She choked her pain inside herself. As an adult, her belief that she has defects and shortcomings leads her to be a perfectionist, and pushes her to stay in an unhealthy relationship with a man who takes advantage of her financially, maintaining an oppressive and sometimes angry attitude. And when Mary has children, they will assimilate the dysfunctional and codependent models of the parents, they will learn to stifle their own feelings and will tend to constantly prove their worth and fear of being rejected by others.

I don't want to be like my parents

Many adults, children of alcoholics, or people who have experienced violence and chaos in their families as children grow up with an intense urge to behave differently, trying to be a different parent for their children and not to repeat the mistakes of their children.

This is in fact possible. With the right support, the right resources and the necessary determination, you can change. However, dispositions acquired in childhood are hard to overcome. It is necessary to work against an unconscious tendency to re-propose the type of parenting that has been experienced.

You tend to raise your children the way you were raised

The tendency to repeat the parenting style of one's parents is not intentional. It is what you are most familiar with. It is the way in which one has been trained and educated. D.

as a child, you may have vague notions, starting from watching television programs or observing what happens in friends' homes, that other parenting strategies exist. But even a strong will to change may not be enough. You have to change your codependency patterns and learn to think and act differently.

Parenting is difficult and challenging

Most parents would perhaps agree that parenting is a thousand times more difficult than expected.

No matter how much you prepare in advance, no one is completely ready for the challenges of parenting. And parenting also brings additional challenges for children of alcoholics and anyone who has experienced childhood trauma or emotional neglect if they don't have a role model for exercising functional parenting.

All parents need a great deal of support and self-love. They need practical help (babysitters, neighbors who will give kids a ride to training camp, and so on) and emotional support (an encouraging friend, empathic family members) to help them get through the ups and downs of parenting. It really takes an enlarged circle of people, a "parental tribe" to raise a boy. And if the family of origin is dysfunctional, a parent will likely intentionally want to broaden their circle of support by connecting with other moms and dads who share their parenting values and goals.

Everyone makes mistakes; no one is a perfect parent. Therefore, always be understanding with yourself and forgive yourself when you are wrong.

Break the circle of codependency

If you want to break the cycle of codependency, the first step is acceptance. Denial is strong in codependent families: it can be painful to recognize and cope with the damage that has been done to oneself and, in addition, to have reproduced the circle. It is important to work with a therapist who understands codependency and the trauma at its source, because this is challenging work, often beyond an individual's ability to process and heal on their own.

Talk about feelings. In dysfunctional families, children are not allowed to express their feelings, so they are repressed. This can contribute to the onset of mental and relational problems. You can break this pattern by showing your children that you are interested in knowing their feelings and accepting them. Children need help learning to pay attention, to properly identify and express their feelings. You can start by regularly asking your children how they are feeling, responding to them with empathy (example: "this must be really hard for you!"). In an age-appropriate way, you can also tell them how it feels. If you still have young children, you can have them use a drawing with pictures representing the different feelings, so that they can point them out, or watch movies like Inside Out with them.

Have realistic expectations. It is very common for parents to think that their children can do things that are beyond their level of development (and then they get frustrated when they don't get it or don't quite make it). This is very likely to happen if you had parents who demanded adult behavior from an early age. If you are not sure what a ten-year-old should be able to do, you need to turn to experts to find out and avoid making the mistake of demanding it.

Allowing your children to have different opinions and beliefs. In other words, kids should be encouraged to be themselves - and not just versions of their parents. A strong sense of self is a great defense against codependency. When children get to know each other and take care of themselves, they are less likely to feel like they have to prove their worth through self-sacrifice and compliance.

Let your children try new things. You can avoid this by giving your children the opportunity to try a variety of activities, meet new people and even take risks.

Praise the children's efforts, not the results. It is natural to want your children to be successful - win a race, get a good grade. However, this can be slippery ground. First, not all kids can excel in school or other traditional fields of success. Praise for achievements can only give kids the message that they are loved and valuable if they achieve that certain result. If, on the other hand, you focus on the children's efforts, you encourage them to persevere, work hard and improve.

Treat your children with respect. Even if your teens don't behave well or annoy you, this is no reason to threaten them, belittle them, hold back love or beat them. Shame can be a drag, but getting help from someone you trust can help contain it and achieve more effective parenting skills.

Set up consistent rules. Children do best when the rules are clear and consistent, yet flexible enough to adapt to their changing needs. It is necessary to avoid the extremes of very hard or too light rules, or to establish rules but not to apply them.

Define healthy boundaries. Borders are where we say "yes" and "no" to someone; they show others what they can expect from us and how they can treat us. You can show your child that it is right to say "no" and not allow others to abuse him. Healthy boundaries can be strengthened by explaining how and why impassable limits must be established. It is also important to respect the boundaries of your children. As children grow, they achieve greater autonomy and the ability to set their own boundaries. However, in most cases, even very young children should have the ability to set their own physical boundaries, for example by deciding whether or not they want to hug someone.

Spending quality time together. Strong family bonds are built when having fun and engaging in meaningful activities together. Try to prioritize family time on a regular basis.

Show them unconditional love. It is not enough to feel the love for one's children; it is necessary to express it in words and deeds. Love can be expressed with a hug, helping them with their most difficult homework, reading them a story before they fall asleep, spending the afternoon together or telling them for example: "I 'm very happy that you are my child!".

Ultimately, for a parent, taking care of themselves and trying to overcome their codependency is the most important thing they can do to break this vicious circle , laying the foundations for a healthy educational and emotional relationship with their children and avoiding transferring them. Their own insecurities.

PARENT-CHILD ADDICTION

First, a diagnosis of "parent or child emotional dependence" does not exist in official psychiatry and psychopathology. Almost always , those who suffer from this type of problem ask for help from a specialist only when the disorder has translated into a language compatible with the medical one, that is, it has become "depression", "anxiety", "anorexia", bulimia "," phobia and / or compulsion ". As is found in all other addictions, including drug addictions, those who experience an emotional dependence on a parent or child tend to deny that they have a problem and resist outside help to the end of their strength. Only the emergence of a recognizable pathology brings the issue of affective dysfunction to the attention of specialists, and this happens belatedly, when the addiction has acquired total control of the behavior, thoughts and emotions of the subjects it involves.

More than what occurs in love addiction, in parental affective dependence, the "sick" is always at least two: mother and daughter or son and, less frequently, father-daughter. In some cases, addiction can involve the entire father-mother-child triad, all unwittingly advocating a vicious circle. The two or more individuals subjected to this type of bond, without realizing it, and driven by the best intentions, cooperate in building a maze that imprisons everyone, but who requires a psychotherapeutic support is usually the child /a.

The co-dependent parent, on the other hand, tends, in the worst case, to refuse help, to devalue it or openly denigrate the validity or usefulness of professional support; at best, the co-dependent parent "allies" with the therapist to "help" him in the care of his sick child, in an unconscious attempt to take the place of the specialist so as to avoid his help. Both attitudes of the dependent parent aim to deny their participation in the problematic scheme and, above all, to conceal their own problem: dependence on the child.

A child who is emotionally dependent on his mother or father often expresses only a part of much wider and longer-term difficulties, relating to the history of the parents, the relationship they have with their families of origin and the system of values to which they refer to. Dependent parents, beyond the specificity of the individual case, are united by a complex of beliefs, emotions and behaviors:

- Anxiety and pessimism;

- Serious problems in the relationship with the spouse;

- Moral rigidity.

THE FACTORY OF COMPLACENCY: HOW A PATHOLOGICAL NARCISSISTIC PARENT RAISES FUTURE CODEPENDENTS

Pathologically narcissistic parents cling to the fantasy that having a child will completely transform their life. Due to their inherent narcissism, they believe that the way they will raise their baby - which they convince themselves will be the perfect cherub - will prove to their friends and family that critical and unfair judgments against them were wrong. If they raise the "perfect" child, it means that they are "perfect" parents and therefore finally their worth and dignity will be demonstrated to the world.

Because pathological narcissists have a base of shame and self-loathing and are eager to be loved and appreciated, they rely on their child to feel capable and valuable. Therefore, the child is overburdened with the responsibility to validate and reaffirm the narcissistic parent. As a result, this child is deprived of the development of a healthy identity, as he is forced to become an extension of the parent's damaged ego. The child then becomes the balm for the emotional wounds of the pathological narcissistic parent.

The pathologically narcissistic parent mistakenly believes that by bringing a new life into the world, he will be able to heal his own childhood wounds and correct the mistakes of his traumatic past. Thus, in an unrealistic way, the child is overloaded with the responsibility of undoing and healing the psychologically impaired childhood of the father or mother. Although a pathological narcissist believes he can offer a child the support and protection he never had for himself, he is unable to do so by virtue of his disorder. Although this father or mother believes in the one-dimensional fantasy that love, in itself, is enough and advances to raise a healthy child, his own lack of introspection and psychological skills nullifies this possibility in the bud, so that the dream of becoming a parent capable of affirming, nurturing and loving collides with reality. Paradoxically, this father or mother unknowingly transfers his dark, insecure and unstable past to his innocent and unprotected child.

Consequently, the artificial burden of behaving so that the parent feels good about himself is placed on the child of the pathological narcissist.

Since it is impossible for any child to satisfy narcissistic parental needs and fantasies, they will naturally be prone to stress and anxiety from the earliest years of life. To deal emotionally with the narcissistic parent, the child will try to adapt to the style of interaction and emotional needs that are neither natural nor appropriate to his stage of development. If he successfully adjusts to the parent's narcissism, then he will be perceived as the complacent and willing child who will help him fulfill the fantasy of being good.

Ultimately, codependency is forged by the child's efforts to independently secure conditional love and attention, pleasing the narcissistic parent while playing the unrealistic role he was unfairly entrusted with at birth. The child who is able to make the narcissistic parent feel good about himself and who conforms to his or her fantasies is likely to be the recipient of conditional praise and love, while the child who cannot or does not want to conform to the narcissistic needs of the pathological parent will be subjected to a much more severe and possibly abusive treatment. What causes codependency to develop in place of Narcissistic Personality Disorder is simply the child's ability to make the narcissistic parent feel at their best.

Alice Miller, in her book The Drama of the Gifted Child (1979), described the child's unique emotional bond with his pathological narcissistic parent. The Dr. Miller used the term "gifted child" to describe children who are able to deal with the education selfish, self-centered and narcissistic parent reactive developing strategies coping intricate but effective. According to Dr. Miller, the narcissistic parent is an emotionally immature and psychologically damaged individual who uses conditional and manipulative parenting practices to satisfy his or her self-centered and selfish needs for attention, validation and acceptance.

Some children of narcissistic parents survived the harsh reality of their formative years by indulging their one-dimensional fantasy of the parent-child relationship. The "gifted" child, who could convince the narcissistic parent to care for him, would be cared for appropriately. Intuitive, or "gifted" children as Alice Miller called them, successfully adapt to the conditioned and harmful upbringing of their narcissistic parents by developing accurate and automatic protective responses.

Since the parents, especially the mother, are the child's only source of survival, he strives to please her for fear of being disapproved or abandoned. The roles are reversed and the child often takes the parent's responsibility to be the emotional caretaker. This prevents the growth of the child's true identity and often results in "loss of self".

Dr. Miller described how, from childhood, the child of a narcissistic parent intuitively understands and adapts to narcissistic needs and expectations. The child learns to relegate his own needs to the background in his unconscious mind to maintain an artificial sense of psychological equanimity. She learns to have a sensitivity and adaptation to the idiosyncratic and unpredictable ups and downs of her narcissistic and emotionally unstable mother or father. For this reason it is able to create a sense of predictability, security and, ultimately, emotional self-reliance. Although this child are essentially denied their basic feelings of safety and security - as the needs of narcissistic parents are increasingly critical of his - he still enjoys conditioned forms of love and appreciation that he is given.

THE NARCIST'S COMPLIENT SON

By learning to be a complacent or gifted child, the child ensures at least the crumbs of positive attention from the parents. Since this baby arouses positive attention from others, it will serve to make parents feel joy and pride. In the long run, this child is incorporated into the parent's ego, as everything he does has an impact on the parent. Instead of being a wonderful, lovable child simply because he exists, he becomes a valuable acquisition or some kind of trophy that demonstrates the value and importance of the parent to others.

Since the child is considered an extension of his narcissistic parent, there is not much difference between the compliments the narcissist receives for his looks, a piece of jewelry, his car, or his adorable and gifted son. All are treated as objects of the pathological narcissist, whereby the individuality of the complacent child is absorbed by the insatiable need of the pathological narcissist to draw attention to him.

The child destined to become codependent is likely a docile child, who automatically and constantly behaves in a way that makes the pathologically narcissistic parent feel full and capable. That child, destined to become codependent, soon learns that conditional love is better than no love . Also learn that there is an inherent risk of disappointing and angering the mother or father and thereby becoming a recipient of the parent's narcissistic anger.

The choice between love and the adulation of the parent against his anger and mistreatment is clear to this child. He has invested a lot to perfect his "pleasant" qualities. Future codependents develop a behavioral instinct to be perceived as exemplary children. They quickly learn the benefits of staying true to the likeable and talented characters they have created. Children always become complacent or kind at the right time. However, to keep the costume with the perfect baby's identity in order, you need to betray yourself. For example, they smile when they want to cry, they remain calm when they are afraid, they obey when they want to rebel, and they behave lovingly when they are angry and resentful.

NARCISISTIC WOUNDS

For the complacent / gifted child, much depends on their ability to respond quickly and appropriately to the rapidly fluctuating emotional states of the pathological narcissistic parent. If this child makes a miscalculation and disappoints or even embarrasses the parent, he will most likely be hurt by the narcissist and will consequently be a witness or victim of his anger.

After the wrath disaster of a person with a narcissistic personality disorder, they often feel extreme resentment of you for making them lose control. He may also shut you out for a period of time by refusing to talk about the incident again. (Payson, 2002, p. 24).

Narcissistic anger manifests itself on a continuum ranging from withdrawal and expressions of mild irritation or annoyance to severe outbursts, including violent attacks (Malmquist, 2006)

To avoid triggering a narcissistic wound and subsequently becoming the target of the pathological parent's narcissistic rage, the complacent / gifted child develops finely tuned radar that quickly and accurately picks up potentially dangerous emotional situations. It is an extraordinary tracking system because it is tuned with such precision that it detects the most subtle changes in a pathological narcissist's emotions or mood - from barely noticeable or hidden ones, to indignation or anger. Predicting parents' emotional states, identifying their triggers, and going unnoticed prevents humiliation, emotional deprivation and potential harm. He will learn that his needs will never be as important as those of the pathologically narcissistic parent and the other narcissists who will eventually appear in his life.

To learn how to go unnoticed and emotionally survive his narcissistic parents, the child must learn to separate from his feelings. Without this separation, the child would come to the emotional certainty that he is not worthy of unconditional love and that he lacks intrinsic importance and value.

To experience the full extent of his feelings, such as humiliation, fear of aggravated harm, anger or despair, would be too much of a blow to his young and fragile mind. So , by pushing those feelings, thoughts and memories into the unconscious mind, or by repressing the emotionally evocative events, the child's psyche defends itself against what it is unable to handle or process.

Repression is an unconscious strategy or defense mechanism that protects the human mind or brain from the harmful effects of trauma.

STRATEGIES FOR INCREASING YOUR SELF-ESTEEM

Self-esteem is the evaluation we give ourselves, the way we live there. Since psychologists has been defined in many ways, even complex ones, such as "self-concept", "personal skills", " self-perception ", but we all know that according to our own self-worth depends on many things. How many times have we heard of us saying "you don't trust yourself", "you are not aware of your potential", or "who do you think you are" ... all self-esteem problems!

Self-esteem is determined by objective and subjective information, referring to three types of self:

- Real self: it is the objective evaluation of our skills

- Perceived self: it is our evaluation of the real self. It is difficult for the perceived self and the real self to coincide, there is always the risk of making "errors of evaluation"

- Ideal self: it is how we want to be. It is influenced by culture and society.

Problems related to self-esteem arise from the discrepancy between the ideal self and the perceived self. If we tend to devalue ourselves, we feel too far from what we want to be, our ideal model appears to us too far and unattainable, and we suffer from it. On the contrary, people who overestimate themselves are convinced that they are what they want, they have reached their ideal, but this is more their opinion.

The concept of self-esteem is not unitary but refers to different areas:

- Social: it is related to the circle of friends and acquaintances, to the relationship with the partner. It is about how we are when we are with others, if we feel approved, supported, helped...

- School / work: how good we feel in starting an activity and the advantages that this entails: good grades, career, satisfaction...

- Family: is influenced by emotional security. In children, the mother-child relationship and parental evaluations are salient

- Body: it is linked to physical appearance and physical performance.

Self-esteem influences self-efficacy, that is the awareness of being able to achieve goals, influences the mood, emotional relationships, in general, influences success in life and choices of all kinds. Some mental illnesses are heading to affect self-esteem, just think of depression, due to which the patient is despised and is devalued, or mania, for which the patient feels a very important person.

Psychotherapists help patients with problems related to self-esteem with a special training, deciding on which of the three aspects of the self is more appropriate to work:

- Patients who need an intervention on the real self, are generally people with few skills, it is good to teach them communication skills, solve problems... in short, develop their potential to the fullest. Let's think of the case of a very shy boy who thinks girls don't like him: the intervention will be aimed at improving his social skills to successfully manage interpersonal relationships.

- When there is a tendency to undervalue oneself excessively, it is better to intervene on the perceived self by helping the person to objectively examine their competences, reporting facts that go against false beliefs. For example, an anorexic that refuses to eat because she sees fat needs intense work on the correct perception of her body image.

Better to focus on the correction of the ideal self if the patient wants to reach goals that are really excessive for him. It's about helping him understand where his ideals come from and helping him resize them, as in the case of a teen-ager who feels failed because she would like to be a model but is too short.

THE CONCEPT OF SELF-ESTEEM

The "concept of self" and "self-esteem" have received considerable attention in the psychological literature, considering that thousands of studies have been conducted on these two constructs. However, despite this mass of studies, a lack of clarity emerges due to the fact that often "self-esteem" and "self-concept" are used interchangeably. It is therefore necessary to specify the meaning of these two concepts.

The concept of self is the constellation of elements to which a person refers to describe himself. It covers all knowledge about the self, such as name, race, likes and dislikes, beliefs, values and physical descriptions (height and weight). For example, a person can see himself as a worker, as Marco's friend, as a person interested in science fiction, and so on; these would all be components of his self-concept.

Self-esteem is instead an evaluation of the information contained in the concept of self; it is the emotional reaction that people experience when they observe and evaluate different things about themselves and it is related to personal beliefs about skills, abilities, social relationships, and future results.

The concept of self-esteem and the concept of self are therefore linked but different; Furthermore, although the self-esteem is connected with the concept of self, and thus influenced by its content, it is possible for people to believe positive things objectively (as recognize academic skills, athletic, or artistic), but continue not really love him the same . Conversely, it is possible for people to love themselves, and thus have high self-esteem, despite the lack of any objective indicator that supports such a positive view of them. We will see later why.

SOURCES OF SELF-ESTEEM

Self-esteem depends both on internal factors, that is the person's cognitive schemes, on his subjective vision of reality and of himself, and on external factors, such as the successes we obtain and the quality of the "messages" we receive from others people.

William James (1890/1983) defined self-esteem as the relationship between a person's perceived self and his ideal self: the perceived self equals the concept of self, the knowledge of those abilities, characteristics and qualities that are present or absent; while the ideal Self is the image of the person we would like to be. According to James, a person will experience low self-esteem if the perceived self fails to reach the ideal self level. The extent of the discrepancy between how we see ourselves and how we would like to be is in fact an important sign of the degree to which we are satisfied with ourselves. In other words, according to James' definition, self-esteem would be the result of the comparison between concrete successes and corresponding expectations:

$$\text{Self-esteem} = \text{Success} / \text{Expectations}$$

However, environmental factors, interacting with the individual, also contribute to improving or worsening performance.

In fact, people develop an idea of themselves on the basis of how they are treated or seen by others: "others mirror us, and we tend to see ourselves as they see us, to judge us as they judge us". In other words, what others think of us, that is the image of us that they send back to us, gradually becomes what we think of ourselves.

But if it is true that what others think of us influences what we think of ourselves, the inverse is also true, namely that others are equally influenced by our judgment about ourselves and tend to see ourselves as we see ourselves. . In fact, there is no more truthful cliché than that according to which "To please others we must first of all please ourselves".

DIMENSIONALITY OF THE CONCEPT OF SELF-ESTEEM

Since the concept of self and self-esteem necessarily correlated to important aspects of our life (e.g. work, friendship, sport, etc.), a person's overall or global self-esteem will depend on the various contexts in which he finds himself. act, but above all by the importance it attaches to each of the components.

Some scholars in fact distinguish "global self-esteem" from "specific self-esteem", defining the first as an overall judgment on one's own value and the second as a judgment concerning a particular self-evaluation sector (physical, intellectual, moral, social, etc.).

However, global self-esteem does not necessarily correspond to the sum or average of the various specific self-esteems. In fact , there are those who, despite reaping successes almost everywhere (and having many specific good self- esteems), are afflicted by a fundamental and generic contempt for themselves; and vice versa there are those who are quite proud of themselves despite having many rather mediocre specific self- esteems.

This is because people assign a different weight to each sector; so the more important it is for a person to be able to evaluate himself well in a given field, the more that specific self-esteem will affect (positively or negatively) his overall self-esteem (e.g. if I am a brilliant painter, but for me to be successful in this field has little value, my overall self-esteem will benefit little).

THE DYNAMICS OF CAUSE AND EFFECT

Positive self-esteem is considered by many to be the central factor of a good socio-emotional adjustment. Having good self-esteem makes it safer, happier, more desirable in the eyes of others and helps us to respond adequately to the challenges and opportunities of life.

In fact, self-esteem seems to be linked to various areas, including psychological health (e.g. depression has been linked to a cognitive style that involves an excessively critical and negative evaluation of the self) and performance (e.g. numerous researchers have found a positive correlation between good self-esteem and higher grades in school).

However, we cannot be sure that high self-esteem is the cause of good performance, or that the opposite is true, i.e. that good performance is the cause of high self-esteem, but causality is likely to work in both directions. : a) the impression one has on one's performance influences one's self-assessments; b) the beliefs that an individual has about himself have a strong impact on the effectiveness of his performance.

In other words, self-esteem can be both a cause and an effect of good or bad functioning in specific areas of the personality.

PROFILES OF HIGH AND LOW SELF-ESTEEM

Self-esteem is not a reflection of people's abilities, in the sense that people with high self-esteem are not necessarily more gifted (intelligent, competent, attractive) than those with low self-esteem. What sets them apart are their beliefs about their abilities, their attitude towards life's trials, their reactions to successes and failures, their social behavior.

People with a globally high self-esteem, in fact, tend to be optimistic and manage to manage negative events with serenity; on the contrary, people with low self-esteem tend to be pessimistic, easily develop depressive crises and are unable to exploit their potential to cope with negative events.

The profiles of high and low self-esteem in relation to actual expectations and performance are outlined below.

EXPECTATIONS

People with high self-esteem before starting any activity, solving a problem, facing a test, generally appear confident and are convinced that they have a good chance of success. Often, in fact, they have a history of previous successes that feed their wildest expectations, but also when in the past I ran into some disappointment compared to similar tasks, they tend to think that "this time will be fine." For these subjects difficult situations and trials are stimulating, they are a challenge to be taken to prove to themselves and to others that they are smart. Furthermore, what they want is not simply to be able to get away with it, but to excel, they want to stand out and surpass their previous results, conquering ever higher goals. To use a scholastic metaphor, they have already achieved a "good" and aim for the "best".

People with low self-esteem find themselves in the opposite situation: before each test, they feel anxious and worried; they would really like to "run away". They have many doubts about the outcome of their efforts, they do not have confidence in their abilities, after all, past experience does not suggest favorable predictions, and therefore they already imagine the moment in which they will have to deal with yet another failure. But even when an initial positive result should encourage them to hope, they panic. They therefore do not see the tests as stimulating challenges, but as threats to their self-esteem, occasions in which they risk proving that they are not capable, interesting and intelligent enough. Given these fears, they certainly do not aspire to exceptional achievements, it would be enough for them to get away with it, not make a fool of themselves, return to the average, not be too inadequate.

People with high self-esteem therefore play "offense" and are optimistic, while those with low self-esteem play "defense" and are pessimistic.

ACTUAL PERFORMANCE

The achievements of people with high self-esteem will be far more numerous and elevated than those of people with low self-esteem due to the degree of commitment and persistence they put into the goals they set.

In fact, people with high self-esteem, despite being satisfied with themselves, often work hard to improve their areas of weakness, while people with low self-esteem, being led to "give up the game" before it is even over, tend to commit little, to be overcome by anxiety and not to persist in their efforts if the first attempts are ineffective.

We see the wickedness of others because we know it through our behavior. We never forgive those who hurt us because we think we will never get their forgiveness. We tell others painful truths because we want to hide them from ourselves. We show our strength, so that no one can grasp our fragility. Therefore, whenever you find yourself judging a brother, be aware that you are on trial.

Let's not lie, you can't suddenly improve self-esteem by reading a book or following the latest quantum transformative technique; self-confidence must be built one step at a time.

In this chapter we will follow this path: a clear and direct path aimed at increasing one's awareness of self-confidence.

Low self-esteem? Here's how to figure it out

The first step is to understand if you suffer from low self-esteem.

If you've ended up in this article, you feel like you have a low opinion of yourself, so you've already made your diagnosis.

However, you can confirm that you have low self-esteem if you often tell yourself:

I'm not up to it

Others don't consider me

It was my entire fault this time too

I'm too ... "bad thing"

I am a goat

Do not the lighthouse never ever

Other signs of low self-esteem can manifest in our relationships, particularly if you have these feelings in the company of other people:

Feeling of general inferiority

Feeling that others know more and more about you

Feeling of always being called into question for negative things

Feeling of being inadequate

Feeling of not being witty, talkative or nice

If you find yourself thinking the above phrases often or experience these annoying sensations often, then you probably suffer from low self-esteem.

The good news is that improving self-esteem is possible and consequently it is possible to detoxify from these unpleasant sensations.

The path to follow could be long and tortuous and requires some consistency, but once you have a satisfactory level of self-esteem, the feeling you get is truly incredible.

THE IMPORTANCE OF HAVING SELF-ESTEEM

For people who do not esteem themselves, success is zero, failure is double.

Self-esteem determines our potential and our ambitions.

If you have low self-esteem you will not aim very high because you will not have confidence in your abilities, while if you have good self-esteem you will increase your potential dramatically.

Moreover, suffering from low self-esteem you will always find yourself unable to seize important opportunities that will happen to you and you will not even be able to create opportunities for yourself and for the people around you.

Generally, those who do not have self-esteem adequate to their possibilities suffer from:

Chronic indecision

He doesn't appreciate his own talents

It magnifies the abilities of others

He tends to avoid opportunities

He is very anxious and passive

He hardly takes the initiative

He feels his opinions ignored when he is able to express them

He has a poor self-assessment

He often thinks he is ignorant

He thinks he's a hardly interesting person

He feels like he can't control his life

When he receives a compliment he thinks it is exaggerated or false

Has difficulty in relating to people, especially of the opposite sex

The fear of making a mistake holds him back

On the other hand, people who have good self-esteem or in any case proportionate to their abilities:

They manage stress and anxiety better

They freely and calmly express their opinion

They know they can do well and have a lot of room for improvement

They are not afraid to relate to others

They are stimulated to learn new skills

They feel good about themselves

They know their weaknesses without making a drama of it

They are not afraid of challenges and on the contrary, sometimes they look for them

They follow their philosophy of life not giving a damn about the thoughts of others

They willingly collaborate with other people

They are committed to achieving what they want

They are responsible for their actions

They leverage their strengths by enhancing them

They defend their opinion but are willing to change it

They know they're not perfect but they are fine with themselves

As you can see, living with an ideal level of self-esteem or living with self-esteem under your shoes makes a big difference and if you are one of those who feel low self-esteem within them you know very well what I'm talking about.

These prospects of improving your quality of life overall by reaching a better level of self-esteem should be enough to induce you to make a change in your life, perhaps not just in regards to self-confidence.

A parable that changes everything

Before continuing with the article, I propose a short story that helps us better define self-esteem and the value we give to ourselves and to the people around us.

"One day, a young man went to see a wise man and said to him:" Please help me: everyone tells me that I am a failure and a fool and it torments me that they are right. "

The wise man looked at him and hastily replied: "Sorry, but I'm in a hurry, I can't help you: I have an important matter to deal with."

Then he paused and added thoughtfully, "But if you want to help me, I'll return the favor."

"Of course, master!" The young man accepted, although he regretted that once again, and moreover by the wise old man, what concerned him was dismissed as something unimportant.

"Well," agreed the sage and slipped a small ring with a beautiful gem off his finger.

"Take my horse and go downtown to sell it: I need it urgently to pay all my debts, so make sure you get a good price.

If it's less than a gold coin don't accept. Go and come back as soon as possible! "

The young man did so, and when he arrived at the market square he showed it to several merchants, who all showed a lot of interest at first.

As soon as they heard that he was selling it only in exchange for gold, however, they immediately became disinterested: indeed, some laughed at him, others, even went away out of the blue.

A merchant told him openly that a gold coin was too much for such a ring, and he would be lucky to get one of copper or at most silver.

Hearing these words, the young man was deeply embittered and, defeated, climbed back into the saddle to return to the sage.

"Master, I am appalled, but I did not succeed: ce l ' would have made for a few silver coins, but I sold it because you told me not to do it for less than a gold coin! But they told me this ring isn't worth that much. "

"Indeed you raise a very interesting question, my boy," replied the sage.

"In fact it would be a really good idea to figure out what it's worth before selling it! And who can make a more accurate estimate than a jeweler?

Get back on horseback and go to the jewelry store to find out how much it's worth. But don't sell it to the jeweler! Ask him as an expert how much he is worth and then come back to me immediately".

The young remounted and reached the jeweler, which long examined the ring under the lens of magnification and carefully weighed.

Finally, he replied to the young man: "Tell your teacher that right now I can't give him more than 58 gold coins, but if he gives me some time to provide, I'll buy it for 70 gold coins."

"70 gold coins?" The young man asked amazed, and ran to the sage at maximum speed.

When the sage heard what the young man told him, he observed: "Remember, my boy: only a true expert can appreciate true value.

So why waste time wandering around the market asking and accepting any fool's opinion? "

Did you like the story? Did you understand the meaning? We do not leave anyone the opportunity to evaluate our worth.

I await your opinion in the comments, now let's see the 5 things you need to know about self-esteem.

To learn how to increase self-esteem a little at a time you have some theoretical concepts to learn to recognize and become aware of its existence and how it works.

Having good self-esteem is not an age factor. It doesn't matter if you are 20 or 80, self-esteem is independent of age. Age is also unrelated to the ability to improve self-confidence, in short, whatever your starting point, you can choose to improve self-confidence.

Self-esteem is important for making decisions. The decisions you make in life, even the smallest ones, are influenced by your level of self-esteem: low self-confidence often translates into lower quality choices with a very low rate of challenge and growth. If you want to have a wider and more stimulating range of choice, it is important to achieve a good level of self-esteem.

The level of self-esteem that a person displays affects everything they think, say and do. Understanding by eye if a person suffers from low self-esteem is not easy, however people with an ideal level of self-esteem are generally more active, disciplined and with a lot of desire to build. Try to look around, those who do not suffer from low self-esteem manage to achieve better results and have no difficulty in relating.

It doesn't matter where you start from. It doesn't matter if you start from a low, medium or near perfect level of self-esteem; self-confidence can be improved and increased regardless of your starting level, in short, no excuses.

Successful people are successful first of all because they consider themselves capable of reaching a higher level. By considering yourself capable of doing and creating, you will enter a virtuous circle where every goal you can conceive and imagine can turn into a real and achievable goal. The more you think you are capable of achieving an ambitious goal, the more energy you will release to achieve it.

How to increase self-esteem without messing up

1 Your appearance: the truth that charlatans don't dare to tell you

All the self-esteem gurus tell you this, but they don't explain effectively how physical appearance affects self-confidence.

Whether we like it or not our appearance affects self-esteem, the sooner you accept this fact, the sooner you will be able to increase your self-esteem.

Let's make some things clear:

Appearance is one of the parameters when evaluating a person, not the only one

The appearance affects your self-esteem because it affects what you think of you the same

A well-groomed appearance sends positive signals to your brain

Taking care of your physical appearance alone won't make you a self-esteem super hero

As I said, you don't have to focus everything on your appearance to increase your self-esteem otherwise there is the risk of becoming inflated balls without self-confidence.

However, it is necessary to consider the external appearance as a parameter that, together with the others, can help improve self-esteem.

It also seems obvious to me that putting on an evening dress to stay indoors and watching television is not necessary and the fact that you don't dress well when alone doesn't mean that self-esteem comes from other people.

It simply means that if necessary you can take care of yourself.

So the lesson to take home is that only the mass thinks that aesthetic self-esteem is the only important one, instead you accept that it exists but don't focus only on it.

So improve your appearance, not trying to achieve non-existent perfection, but a better version of yourself even on the outside.

Aesthetic self-esteem depends on the experience we have of ourselves, for this reason there are insecure models or not very attractive people who are extremely self-confident.

To tell you mine, I find people who think superficial:

That the outward appearance is the only thing that matters and they focus only on that

That the inner aspect is the only thing that matters and they mock those who sweat to have a beautiful physique

There is no need to go around it, both aspects matter, so it is a good thing to try to cultivate both .

But then why do charlatans insist on promoting the fact that the outer appearance doesn't matter at all while the inner one is everything?

Because it serves to give a quick and painless sop to those who do not want to take care of their appearance and as human beings we tend to be lazy, consequently this strategy easily takes root on the mass.

2 How to raise self-esteem with the anchoring technique

Recent studies have shown that our brain cannot exactly define the difference between a truly lived experience and an experience imagined and visualized with great intensity.

The same chemical reactions take place in our body whether we are thinking about something amazing we have done or if we just imagine it vividly.

To exploit this sort of bug we can use the anchoring technique.

The anchoring technique is also used by successful sportsmen and entrepreneurs, here's how to proceed.

Sit back, visualize and perceive a moment in your life when you felt full of energy, when you were at the top of your performance and enthusiasm. Try to relive this moment by recalling all the positive feelings you have experienced.

Hold this good feeling for a few seconds and fix it in a gesture such as closing a hand into a fist and standing up at the same time.

Repeat for at least 5 times to make your brain anchor the pleasant sensations to the movement you have chosen.

Whenever you want to release new energies sit and stand up closing your fist.

This technique works very well if you connect a very strong experience and if you repeat it very often, ideally every day.

It is also a great way to unlock extra energy in the short term to give you a rush of positivity when you need it, but keep in mind that in the long run there are better measures, like the first point we have already seen and the next ones you will read.

Anchoring is a real NLP technique, a discipline that I don't love, but as always, you can try it and if it doesn't work with you, discard it mercilessly.

3 plays on your skills and takes action

One of the most effective ways to improve self-esteem is to work on your skills, in this way the confidence in yourself will start from the inside and not from the outside.

As we have seen, one of the unpleasant sensations that you have when you suffer from low self-esteem is to think that you do not have relevant things to say and consequently perceive your words as not very useful, stimulating and pleasant in the eyes of others.

To remedy this type of problem you have two solutions:

To enhance your experience and your skills specific

Expand your range of skills if you are not particularly competent

If you already have relevant skills or experiences in your life, the only thing you need to do is learn from your past and value what you have learned.

For example, I know people who have made several trips but on balance have not absorbed anything useful from what they have experienced.

In this case it is about increasing your awareness, because if you understand that what you do has value, you increase your self-esteem.

Warning: enhancing your experiences does not mean bragging or constantly bringing them up.

If, on the other hand, you think and feel that you have nothing interesting to say, that you do not know any subject thoroughly, gain experiences, acquire new skills and increase your level of competence.

Try asking yourself: what is the training that could lead me to reach the level I want?

If you think about it there are plenty of successful people who don't have great intelligence, personality or charisma.

However, what really sets them apart is their particular ability, they can do damn well one thing that they can most of the time.

Maybe they too have flaws, paranoia and difficulties, but they value their skills and leverage those.

By becoming truly proficient in a certain field, not only can you benefit from the inherent benefits it brings, but you will be sending out strong and positive signals to your mind.

To be more confident without playing a part you really need to have skills and competences, acting a script will inevitably lead you astray.

4 knows your 3 basic rights

When we suffer from low self-esteem we often forget about our fundamental rights, rights that exist regardless of our beliefs and the judgment of others.

We all have:

- The right to exist

- The right to be happy

- The right to be wrong

These 3 rights may seem obvious, however they are sometimes unconsciously forgotten to leave room for a long series of duties, often non-existent, to which we must fulfill.

Knowing your 3 rights is a conscious step to regain confidence in yourself: you must constantly consider yourself authorized to act and above all to make mistakes.

When you have to decide something of important, always listen to your opinion, expect mistakes and accept them.

Thinking that you can make perfect decisions and act perfectly on every occasion is a false and disempowering expectation.

To retroactively make your 3 rights valid, try this exercise to increase your self-esteem: take a pen and paper and write down the events in which you have not felt good about yourself and in which you think that your self-confidence has suffered a hard blow.

Now write down next to each occasion that you consider negative your fundamental right that you did not consider at the time, for example:

Marco told me that I am a bad person and that I will never be happy.

At that party I made a fool of myself in front of everyone, I'm sick just thinking about it.

A possible application of your rights could be:

Marco is not a supreme entity, I have every right to be happy and from now on I will do everything in my power to succeed.

I have the sacrosanct right to make mistakes, nobody is perfect. Maybe I was a little unlucky to have slipped into a place full of people, that's all.

Do this exercise in writing, it is very important to transfer your feelings and emotions on paper to overcome any blows from the past that can affect your self-esteem in the present moment.

To act on your present that will inevitably reflect on the future, you must always keep your rights in mind whenever you make decisions or take relevant actions.

Also from less importance to the little voice in your brain telling you:

I cannot do it

I don't deserve it

I will never succeed

Can't go wrong

Remember that self-esteem must start from within but it is very useful to select who has the right to judge and advise you.

Leave this to the best people you know and do not leave this power to negative individuals or worse still to the mass: always remember the parable of the ring.

5 The healthy selfishness that boosts self-esteem

Have you ever noticed that on the plane before take-off the employees start that boring talk about the emergency exits and how to insert the oxygen mask?

Maybe you've never noticed a small detail.

The flight attendants clearly say that before helping others you must wear the mask first and possibly only then assist a person who is in difficulty.

When it comes to self - esteem, it is similar: helping others is undoubtedly a noble thought, but before you think about your neighbor, makes sure you have achieved the best for yourself.

Being affected, so to speak, with a healthy and supportive selfishness offers several advantages, including:

We can be stimulated to achieve greater autonomy in all areas of life

We grow more sincere and rewarding relationships

We mature more as people

We develop our skills and abilities to become unique and special

We become more authentic and sincere with ourselves and with others

We develop the will to invest in ourselves thanks to self- love

But why can developing one's healthy selfishness increase self-esteem so much?

Thinking first of yourself and of your own well-being releases us from actions aimed at earning the goodwill of others.

In doing so, we no longer make decisions for others but for ourselves and for our well-being.

So here's how to grow some healthy selfishness related to self-esteem:

Learn to say no and to distinguish who is sincerely asking you for a favor from who is demanding and demanding your time

Focus on the here and now without focusing too much on scruples and any regrets

Remember that you have no obligations to everything and everyone

Raise your awareness to make sensible decisions independent of others

Once you are able to develop your ideal level of selfishness you will see your self-confidence grow without having to think about it again.

QUESTIONS AND ANSWERS ON SELF-ESTEEM

1 What is the etymology of the word self-esteem?

The word self-esteem derives from Self and Esteem and indicates the subjective process that induces a subject to appreciate himself.

2 Why is it important to have good self-esteem?

Self-esteem as we have seen directly determines what we consider ourselves capable of doing, if we do not consider ourselves capable of carrying out a certain action, we will not even try to carry it out when it could fully fall within our possibilities.

3 If I boost my self-esteem, will I become a balloon?

It is a common opinion that self-confidence leads people to become inflated balloons: nothing could be more wrong. The so-called inflated balloons have too much self-esteem, nothing to do with a level of self- confidence compatible with the person we are.

4 How can I increase my self-esteem?

In the article I have exposed some exercises to increase self-esteem, I advise you to start to assimilate well the points we have seen and try to put them into practice.

5 Can self-esteem increase or decrease over time?

The self-confidence we have in ourselves can change according to the negative or positive events that happen to us, however if you suffer from low systematic self-esteem it is good to try to remedy it.

6 Does having too much self-esteem hurt?

Having too much self-confidence means not having inner balance but suffering from an excess that is generally better to balance.

In summary:

- Know what self-esteem is and how it works

- Synchronize exogenous self-esteem with endogenous self-esteem

- Act on your skills and experiences

- Set yourself sensible and achievable goals

- Be aware of your fundamental rights and absorb them

- Remember your successes and learn correctly from mistakes

- Decide who are the people who have the right to judge you

- Re-evaluate and re-dimension your inner voice

- Make comparisons with judgment and objectivity

- Get out of your comfort zone

- Increase your healthy selfishness

- Find the sport that suits you (preferably as a team)

- Do not be afraid to become a balloon inflated

- Get it wrong quickly

- Forget the perfect ideals that don't exist

- Look after your outward appearance as much as you care inward

- Improve your skills

"When you are able to applaud yourself, it is much easier to applaud others"

Denis Waitley

Boosting self-confidence is not a quick and painless process, but a process that takes time and effort, you will have to step out of your comfort zone and expose yourself little by little.

Self-esteem is a very delicate matter but of fundamental importance to be able to act freely and develop our latent potential, it is really worth investing some time at least to take stock of the situation.

CODEPENDENCY RECOVERY PLAN

10 steps to regain serenity and go back to being free

1. Admit you have a problem

The first step to heal is to realize that you have a problem in the way you live romantic relationships, and in general the important bonds in your life. Admitting that you have a wrong attitude in relationships, which does not allow you to live them peacefully and in a rewarding way, is in fact essential to be able to ask for help, or simply question old patterns and old habits that make you suffer. It is the first step towards healing.

2. Get to know each other better

If you no longer know who you are, how are you going to find what you want? Those who suffer from emotional dependence focus on the other give themselves completely to the other and forget about themselves; behaves as if he does not deserve love and attention, as if it is dangerous to present his needs and expectations to the other. In this way he distances himself further and further from himself and no longer knows him, because he no longer listens. It ends up becoming the sum of all the people it is linked to; a copy of the others. Dedicating time to yourself by listening to your inner dialogue, or simply observing yourself and observing your emotions in silence is a great way to get back in touch with the part of yourself that has been forgotten. Meditation, Autogenic Training and Mindfulness techniques represent, in my opinion, very valid tools to start listening and knowing each other again.

3. Focus on yourself

People with emotional addiction tend to place the other above all else. Even of him. They place the desires and needs of others ahead of their own, and in this way they deny themselves joy and gratification, the possibility of being truly known by the other, and they move further and further away from themselves. To the point of no longer knowing who they are , what they want and what they really need. To achieve healing you need to stop and go back to looking within, observing yourself with love and acceptance. We must slowly start asking ourselves: what do I need? What do I really want? What do I no longer want in my life? Bringing the focus of our attention back to ourselves, to our emotions, desires and expectations, will allow us to return to love ourselves, to know and affirm our needs with others.

4. Learn to set limits and boundaries

Those who suffer from emotional dependence, in their need to be loved and approved at all costs, lose sight of their own boundaries and limits that should not be exceeded. Gradually accept less and less respectful behaviors, increasingly offensive attitudes to the point of accepting true psychological or even physical violence. Forget about limiting the other's interference and demands. His personal boundaries are so blurred and blurred that he often no longer recognizes them, and becomes a sort of extension of the other. Thus, the expectations, requests, needs of the other become one's own needs, without there being any awareness of what they really are. It is therefore necessary to LEARN TO SAY NO when inside us it is "no". It is necessary to learn to REDEFINE YOUR BORDERS: establish how far the other can go and draw a defined line beyond which tolerance will not be zero and no more unpleasant, disrespectful or offensive behavior, nor excessive requests will be accepted. If we don't learn to be respected by placing limits on the power of the other, no one will do it for us.

5. Affirm yourself

The affirmation of oneself is a fundamental step to rebuild one's well-being and one's freedom, and it is a process that is based on the consideration we have of ourselves and on our ability to love and respect each other. By learning about our wants and needs, and by learning to set boundaries in relationships with others, we slowly prepare the ground for affirming and fulfilling ourselves. For the emotional addict this is an almost unknown process, since he has not learned to say "no" and has not learned to place himself on the same level as the other. Self-affirmation means choosing who we want to spend our time with, the activities we want to carry out and those that don't interest us, it means choosing how we want to dress and where we want to go when we go out: in a nutshell it means EXPRESS OUR NEEDS WITH COURAGE BUT WITHOUT IMPOSING OR DEMANDING THEM THAN OTHER LI MEET. This process also provides that we accept ourselves for who we are: with our strengths and weaknesses even when this is not convenient for others, and above all - a very difficult step for the emotional employee - it means having the courage to give up the approval of others when we affirm something about us that others do not share, and learning to accept to see that the attitude of others towards us can change as a result of our change. Probably some people - those who exploited us or took advantage of our addiction - will leave, but others will come, ready to love and respect us as we are.

6. Increase self-esteem and confidence

The emotional addict lives in a constant condition of self-denial in order to satisfy the other because - let us remember - he is terrified of abandonment and loneliness and in order to have someone close to him, he is ready to give up on himself. But now that we become more deeply aware, we know our real needs and desires, we realize how much we have been devalued, denied, allowed to be overwhelmed. It is time to take our life back in hand and start doing something for you, even giving up if necessary, to always be approved. Self-esteem arises from the ability to value one's needs, tastes and values, without renouncing them to guarantee the presence of the other. It arises from the ability to concretely do what we like and what gratifies us. We learn to appreciate and honor the being that we are, to see our deep beauty! Freeing ourselves from the armor built on the fear of loneliness will make us freer and bring us more respectful people.

7. Free yourself from guilt and shame

Often the emotional addict, aware of assuming inappropriate attitudes generated by his addiction, is ashamed and acts almost apologizing for existing. He is overcome by a great sense of guilt and shame for the mistakes he cannot stop making. He condemns himself for this "guilt" and mistreats himself inside himself, using words of anger and disappointment. In this way he perpetuates the vicious circle: he feels unworthy of being loved, he assumes attitudes of dependence and low self-esteem, he feels guilty for it, consequently his sense of unworthiness and shame increases, his sense of guilt and the conviction of not deserving anything, and these further increases the addictive behaviors generated by the fear of abandonment. FEELING GUILTY WILL NOT HELP YOU FEEL BETTER OR CHANGE THE STATE OF THINGS: we must give up the sense of guilt and have the courage to change, even if this will alienate some people from us.

8. Develop your own strength

Learning to follow intuition, that faint little voice that tells us when something is wrong, is a very important step for each of us, and it is even more so for the emotional addict. Learning to understand when a situation becomes intolerable and painful and requires too many sacrifices (to yourself first of all) is essential to reverse. To say no. Leave. Taking the risk of facing loneliness and the worst fears associated with it. This courage, however, will set us free, and will allow us to understand that solitude is not an endless void but an opportunity for knowledge and love to be dedicated to oneself. A silent garden in which to cultivate love, deep respect and self-knowledge, to return to the world more complete and stronger. The courage to face this pain makes us strong and increases our self-confidence, which in turn will allow us to make the best choices. To develop our strength we must first have the courage to face the discomfort and our deepest fears.

9. Stop fearing the judgment of others and become "selfish"

Breaking free from the noose of others' judgment is a very important step on the path to personal and relational freedom and well-being. They taught us to fear disapproval, to align ourselves with what others think that we consider important, to support opinions that we do not share, in order to feel "part of the group", not to be alone, not to risk abandonment. But all this leads us only to exasperate a sort of silent and socially accepted "slavery". Instead we learn to say no, to say what we think, to affirm our ideas and our needs. Without fear that we will be pushed away or abandoned for this. Without even expecting others to take charge of it. Simply letting them exist as they are a part of us, our way of manifesting ourselves in the world. We ask for what we want and reject what we no longer want. We think about ourselves and what brings us growth and well-being, rejecting what brings us pain, discomfort, unworthiness. In the face of disapproval we learn to act respectfully and firmly: this is me, and I deserve the same respect and the same consideration that you deserve.

10. Free yourself from the fear of abandonment

I have placed this passage at the end of the list because in my opinion it requires that all the others be built first, so that there are the conditions to work on it. It is in fact an extremely delicate, painful and difficult process to face; the fear of abandonment - in the form it assumes in emotional dependence - is a great bottomless pit, a void without light that devours energy, courage and hope. It has its roots in early childhood, in the relationship with the reference figures (usually parents), and is able to define the relational patterns that we will use with loved ones throughout our life. In some cases, these patterns are healthy and allow the development of the person and the couple but in other cases - as happens in affective employees - they take on unhealthy, pathological and limiting ways. It is not possible to change these patterns (made up of expectations, memories, behaviors and automatic interpretations) quickly and without first having a deep awareness of the way they manifest themselves in our life. It is advisable to seek the help of a professional who can slowly and gently accompany us along this path of knowledge and radical change. However, I remember that these patterns, responsible for the terror of abandonment and for many of the behaviors that the emotional employee carries out to ensure that he is not left alone, can be changed. By reintegrating the healthier aspects and modifying the beliefs responsible for the pathological aspects.

HOW TO GET OUT WITH PSYCHODYNAMIC PSYCHOTHERAPY

Psychodynamic psychotherapy usually requires medium to long- term commitment, but it is one of the most effective approaches to treating emotional addiction.

Along the way, the therapist guides you in exploring the connections between the psyche, personality and cognition and how these affect mental, emotional or behavioral processes at an unconscious level.

Put simply, the therapist helps you to analyze the root of your current addiction problems: this analysis allows you to begin to see the addiction issues as well as the intense fear of abandonment as arising from early relationships with overly controlling parents or parents. Avoidant (or even abusive).

All the symptoms of emotional addiction are seen as elements to be understood, listened to and valued, rather than fight or judge.

The fundamental element is precisely the relationship that is formed between patient / client and therapist.

It will come naturally to you to ask yourself:

But then can a certain emotional dependence towards the therapist also develop?

Absolutely yes.

You may have heard the cynical view expressed by many about the fact that psychotherapists deliberately manipulate their patients / clients by making them dependent emotionally from them.

In fact, many people fear this and believe that emotional addiction in psychotherapy is a bad thing.

In fact, for psychotherapy to be effective, a certain degree of emotional dependence is desirable: patients who suffer a lot or are confused, who have a history of unstable and chaotic relationships can develop certain dependence even for long periods of time.

Think about it:

if your life does not go as you would like, you grew up in a particularly complicated environment and you have never been able to develop a certain emotional capacity or self-awareness you cannot avoid depending on someone to help you increase these skills.

It is certainly not easy to rely on someone, especially after having lived certain experiences, but it is necessary if you want to get out of it and it must be done at your own pace.

Obviously, the therapist must have worked hard on himself so as not to favor an excessive dependence that would lead the patient to maintain his problem and not allow him to develop a healthy autonomy.

HOW TO FREE YOURSELF FROM THE CHAINS OF AFFECTIVE DEPENDENCE AND BECOME EMOTIONALLY INDEPENDENT

We need to understand deeply that to be free from emotional addiction we must undertake a journey back to our True Self.

I understand that this can create a lot of resistance, but I believe it is the only way forward.

This journey has to do with "self-realization" and not with using others to compensate for one's emotional shortcomings.

And it always starts by looking inside.

This is why in this part I have collected from various experts and from my personal experience the 8 essential steps to become emotionally independent both in relationships and in life.

Are you ready?

Let's start!

1) Avoid placing responsibility on others for your happiness

People who can't emotionally look after themselves often look for someone else to do it for them.

But no matter how good someone else makes you feel, it is vital to develop some confidence in yourself and in your abilities.

To learn what is required so much self-observation and practice is definitely not easy but it can help you develop independence and autonomy.

You may have thoughts such as

"Only someone else can make me happy"

"I can't love myself if someone else doesn't love me"

When you think this way, what really happens is that you are making your happiness dependent on that person. A continuous circle of reward and punishment is created.

And the addiction itself makes you unhappy.

An important step on the path of freedom is to allow other people to be free rather than resent their behavior. You can always seek help but you ca n't expect it because in the end no one owes you anything.

Your love for yourself has to be built from within.

Loving yourself is the beginning of a love story that lasts a lifetime

O. Wilde

2) Identify the mechanism of Idealization

Idealization leads us to imagine the other as perfect or to see him on a pedestal: we tend to see above all the positive elements and to deny or justify the negative ones.

This can lead us to give more importance to the wishes of the other rather than our own.

Think about it:

This mechanism always leads you to suffer and not see the other objectively.

In reality, what we subconsciously end up doing is using the other to fill our insecurities and make him the only one who can do it.

The other person feels that they have complete power over us and this can lead them to manipulate us or make us suffer (I have already discussed the connection with the narcissistic individual who is really drawn to addictive personalities before).

3) Learn to take better care of yourself on an emotional level

I have collected some essential points here:

Recognize your needs and make your happiness a priority

Recognize your worth and work on improving your self-esteem: question your negative thoughts about yourself, focus on your strengths and recognize your limitations, work on your goals and begin to understand that you are actually capable of do what's best for you (or get help if you can't).

Observe the behaviors that lead you to attack yourself and gradually replace them with behaviors of understanding and acceptance.

Develop your intellectual curiosity: learn and discover new things about yourself, others and what happens to you. Look for anything you might like.

Learn to calmly observe, watch and fully experience all emotions (even negative ones).

Share and recognize your emotional needs: there is not a single person who can listen to and understand you. Building a circle of friendships or talking to a therapist can be great ways to share what's inside.

When you do something wrong don't be too hard on yourself, always consider it a necessary step in learning new things.

Try to bring your attention to the present moment as much as possible: this practice allows you not to favor too much the rumination of thought, which amplifies more negative emotions and thoughts.

Surround yourself with people who value you and not toxic people who make you suffer.

4) Recognize the destructive patterns stemming from childhood

As already pointed out above, most of the problems of Affective Addiction come from difficult experiences during childhood or adolescence.

Recognizing these events and the way you used to deal with them is a great way to understand why you find yourself experiencing emotional addiction today.

This does not mean getting lost in your past, but exploring the models you have learned (mostly unconsciously) to try to detach yourself from it.

In a certain sense, emotional dependence feeds on itself: we can speak of a vicious circle and self-fulfilling prophecies. I have observed how some patients, despite rationally realizing that they are making a mistake, are unable to do otherwise.

This happens because the models we have built over the years are rigid and do not allow the person to experience himself in a different way.

In a sense, it is necessary to unlearn before you can learn anything new.

The therapy can help a lot in this: a part of the solution is just to learn to distinguish between the situations present and those that have happened in the past. This can also lead to observing and distinguishing between the child we once were and the adult we want to become.

5) Become aware of the fear behind your addiction

A child is unable to understand the addictive patterns that the mind begins to develop in order to survive in childhood.

But many of us keep repeating these patterns even as adults, because we fail first of all to identify them and then to grow beyond them.

There is a lot of fear that hides behind the mask of emotional addiction.

It is strange, but for many of us, the greatest fear is that of being with ourselves, alone with our being. Therefore we constantly try to distract ourselves and the objects of distraction tend to become addictive factors.

The path to freedom lies in letting consciousness take over all of our behavioral patterns and our unconscious emotional experiences.

6) Don't be afraid of loneliness

One of the main reasons addiction develops is the fear of being alone. I have already explored this topic in a dedicated article (inner solitude).

We are constantly looking for some form of entertainment or distraction just to avoid being alone with ourselves.

We are scared of "being" so we continue to "do".

All addiction, or the feeling of incompleteness, exists because we tend to seek satisfaction outside, not within ourselves.

And in solitude we can find all our strength.

If we can deal with this fear, we will be able to see everything beyond.

7) Make it your goal to find out who you really are

Most of us have no idea who he really is, so it ends up to be completely dependent on a self-image that has been built.

The ' self-image, however, is simply an idea that needs content to stay alive. This content is usually provided by others, which is why we always seek them out to define ourselves.

In fact, the main cause of emotional dependence is a negative self-image that has built up over time.

If you want to free yourself from emotional addiction, you should therefore seek who you truly are beyond all these "self-images "that the mind has created.

8) Start working on building well-defined boundaries

One of the basic steps to recover from emotional addiction is to learn to build appropriate emotional boundaries. This is a pretty big topic and I'll probably write a whole article about it.

Loving you: how to really take care of yourself

Loving yourself, learning to love yourself is the way to live a happy life.

If you don't know how to love yourself, you will never be happy. I recommend 4 practical actions tried by me and many other people, always with excellent results.

Love yourself: love yourself or become selfish?

Chances are you've already read a lot of tips to learn how to take care of yourself.

I've done it too and the thing I've learned is that self-care is almost always confused with selfishness.

It almost seems that in order to love yourself you have to give yourself everything, without rules, without savings (even economic!).

Television offers us advertisements in which it seems that you can only take care of yourself by understanding this or that product, as if shopping were enough to learn to love yourself more.

Not everything we consider enjoyable, therefore, is truly self-love.

To help you understand if the treatments you usually give yourself are really valuable, I make a list of what they should never cause:

Addiction. They become things that you can no longer do without without feeling some negative emotion.

Addiction. That is, the more you take, the less it works. The more you give yourself something, the less useful it is, so you end up wanting more and more or feeling dissatisfaction and boredom.

Negative emotions. For example towards people who do not help you, or towards those who seem to prevent you from enjoying it.

If what you do to take care of yourself causes these effects, forget it .

Even if it sounds right, nice, if everyone agrees it's a good thing.

Loving yourself, or yourself, is the way to live a happy life.

Dependence, addiction and negative emotions are always at odds with this goal.

To say this, of course, is easy and it also seems the most obvious thing.

However, I often hear the answer: "And how should I act with love towards myself? How you do it?"

Learning to love each other means first of all learning to love .

What do you do when you love? Some ideas...

You listen with interest to the person talking to you.

Forgive a mistake and try to understand the reasons.

You spend time with this person and you want to know them, understand them.

You respect his ideas; you accept his points of view even if you don't share everything.

These are just some ideas, some gestures we normally perform when we feel love for someone.

They are also obvious and shareable, but the difficult thing is to understand how to direct them towards ourselves.

Love for yourself: isolate yourself and remain silent

This is one of the simplest, most important and most feared things to do.

Take it hard on yourself just by listening to who you are.

Choose a suitable place, where no one can disturb you, eliminate all distractions, do not think about the problems you have to solve and stay there, alone, or alone , with you.

Imagine you want to get to know someone you like, what do you do?

Do you always frequent her in the midst of confusion? Do you always meet her only in the presence of others?

I say no.

You will definitely go out with this person, alone.

You will not be in front of the television, but you will talk, without distractions.

After all, you could be the person you know the least. Then follow these directions:

Get a fixed time every day to yourself, or you own.

Make sure this appointment doesn't include guests.

The appointment must be something of intimate, choose a niche and comfortable.

Eliminate music, television, cell phone or other distractions.

For example, I like to walk alone, listen to the rain under a sheet metal veranda (because it amplifies the sound of water drops), stay in my room, watch the fire in the fireplace, watch the sunrise early in the morning, observe animals, trees, leaves.

The important thing is that there are only you.

No distractions, no rush, don't get caught up in what you'll do next.

You simply have to observe yourself, listen, calm and relax your mind.

A simple thing, as mentioned, but I assure you it will be very effective.

All negative emotions come from fear

Fear is the basis of every negative emotion, and it is the one we feel most often, without perhaps recognizing it.

How to be yourself: accept your mistakes

This is a crucial point, perhaps not easy to think about, but I am convinced that if we commit ourselves we can make it easier.

Understanding how to be yourself and love yourself means accepting your mistakes, and to do so you need to understand how to look at your mistakes.

Here's what I recommend you do.

Write down on a piece of paper the latest mistakes you made, especially the less important ones.

For each, write the reasons why you did, or didn't, that way.

Then write what prompted you to make these choices, what you believed, what you hoped for , what you feared.

Finally, write down what you can do to remedy that error.

The first points will help you understand yourself better.

We often don't recognize the reasons that push us to act.

The last, however, does two things: if you can do something, even for indirect or partial, to correct the mistake, does it.

Now, don't wait until next month.

If, on the other hand, you can't do anything (but it will be very rare!), At least try to treasure the experience.

Then write what that mistake taught you:

What did you learn from this mistake?

How does the way you act in the future change in a similar situation?

What could you do to make your experience useful to others (teach it, share it, tell it)?

How can you be sure, or sure, that you won't make the same mistake again?

Answer all these questions, and write down each answer, because it reinforces what you think and becomes a track that you can access when you need it.

HOW TO LOVE YOURSELF: WHO KNOWS YOU BEST?

Your mother? Your sister? Your husband or your girlfriend? A friend, the best?

No, actually the person who knows you best is you.

You may not always realize it, but this is the truth.

However, you can always improve yourself and become more aware of your personal relationship. Let's see how.

Write your success: a degree, a promotion, a sporting triumph.

Write down the most beautiful human experience you have ever had.

Write your typical day, one of those absolutely routine.

When you write a success think about the qualities that made you achieve it.

Not to feel better, but to understand that they are a part of you that often ends up in the attic.

When you write a touching human experience, look at the human values you have put in place, the capacity for understanding and understanding.

These are also qualities you possess, although often underestimated.

Then when you write your typical day, observe qualities, strengths or weaknesses, the way you do everything, the attitude, the importance of your work or your gestures.

All those things that seem obvious or trivial are a part of you.

This is an easy way to get to know yourself better and respect who you are

Are you capable of living a happy life?

1. Learning to love yourself: where do you live!?

A great way to take care of yourself is to make the environment you live in perfect.

Wait, don't rush.

I know a lot of people, usually women, who are obsessed with order or cleanliness, and almost always because others think well of them.

Loving yourself does not mean winning the house of the year award (does it exist?), But creating an environment in which to live in line with ourselves.

My bed is always unmade, clothes are often on the sofa and my table always has books and sheets often in random order.

But I'm fine with it. Here are some tips.

If you like the order, order everything.

Clutter is a relative concept, but if you live in an environment that bothers you with confusion, then you need to fix things.

Make your home more yours: paint the walls in the colors you prefer, put the paintings you like, move the furniture as you say.

You can tidy up and tidy your home several times, perhaps changing it every month, or twice a year. The important thing is that it is comfortable for you.

Create spaces for reflection, for solitude and for company, to relax, work or study.

Look at your home: would you change it for a more beautiful one?

The last point, in particular, is provocative : beautiful is a relative concept, but you have to create an environment that you would not change with anyone, because it is yours and for you it is the most beautiful and welcoming in the world.

Organize it however you like.

There is no way to paint the walls, there is no right order to arrange your furniture, it is not true that there is a rule on how to order the things you have in the house.

You can do as you like.

Getting rid of patterns and limits is the heart of self-care.

Start from your home, or from your room

2. Lies have short legs

To tell the truth, to be honest, is an act of love for oneself.
Something that is good for you first, as well as for your relationships.

How honest are we with ourselves?

In these years I have understood that you have to learn to be it with yourself, first of all.

What does it mean? Here are some examples:

Don't seek excuses or guilty for your mistakes.

Even if no one sees you doing a wrong thing, you know it, you can't pretend.

Try to understand the real reasons for your actions, do not look for good excuses.

We often tend to look for reasons that others can share.

We don't like being judged, so we often lie to ourselves not to admit that we wanted to do something or that we liked that situation.

Others wouldn't approve, so we can't admit we like it.

You can deceive others, until at some point, but not yourself, or you same : you know the truth, it is inevitable.

Do you know what happens if you repress it, if you pretend you don't see it?

That that truth will make you feel bad, it will create discomfort, negative emotions, fear of it coming out.

In one word: unhappiness.

Being honest, or honest, takes away a lot of trouble, simplifies your life, and quickly becomes a good, positive habit.

You don't have to pretend, you can be natural and that's a big energy saver.

There is no hidden truth that can come up, and that reduces the things that scare you.

You can be consistent and transparent, and this strengthens your ability to understand who you are, your worth and your uniqueness.

Does a person who tells you lies love you?

Sure, maybe he wants to protect you, but do you consider lying to you a gesture of love?

Making decisions for you, deceiving yourself and keeping yourself in the dark about the truth?

Not me, but you might see it differently.

Surely if you want to love yourself, take it hard on yourself, you certainly can't start by making fun of yourself.

Just as being honest is fundamental to those we love, it is, perhaps even more true to ourselves.

Let's get practical, here's what you can do immediately.

Many girls and women dye their hair white, use make-up or dress in a certain way to please others (or not to be misjudged), but (yes) they say they do it because they like it and that they don't care. Judgment of others. Is this your case? Be sincere.

Many guys and men behave arrogantly and aggressively because they are insecure and fear of being belittled, but (yes) they say they do it because they are confident and strong and not to look like it. Is this your case? Be honest.

Almost all of us defend choices and ideas taken because admitting a mistake seems belittling to us and we fear the negative judgment of others, but (to ourselves) we say that it is because we are sure of ourselves and understand more than others who judge superficially. Is this your case? We are sincere!

Being honest often doesn't involve a news story in the city newspaper, but just a change in the way you communicate with yourself, or yourself.

First of all you have to admit that you're taking in around

3. Acting with love: the most important secret

When I read books or sites where it is explained how to love yourself, or if he was, I'll notice something I find counterproductive: the advice is to take care of himself shifting the emphasis from the others.

It almost seems that loving others is an obstacle to loving ourselves. Could it be true?

I honestly don't know a single better remedy than love to feel better.

The last piece of advice is therefore to act with love.

Here's what to keep in mind before we start giving you practical advice.

Loving others does not mean being subjected to them and doing whatever they want.

Loving others does not mean letting us put our feet on our heads or suffer their oppression.

I can't love someone I condemn for the things they do. Nobody is their own mistakes.

To love I must have learned to manage my emotions and understand how they are born.

Loving is a choice that requires strength and courage.

Those who advise against loving, when talking about self-care, do so because, in my opinion, they confuse love with attachment and dependence on others.

When he feels love, he thinks only of a couple, possession, submission.

Act with love towards other people. Simple, kind gestures, without asking for anything.

Show your emotions of love and affection: hug, smile, shake hands, show interest.

Return each offense with a compliment: look for the positive things and forget the others.

Do daily favors for those around you. Go one meter more than others without expecting them to reciprocate or be grateful to you.

Because? What does it have to do with self-care and dedication to others?

I'll explain it to you right away.

What is the thing you could want most of all but love? Am I wrong?

Don't you want to receive love?

Attention, care, interest, respect, listening, forgiveness?

Don't you want others to love you? Why do you want love?

The reason is simple: love is what makes us feel better than anything else.

Here's good news: if you love others, the love you give will be part of your life.

Do you think the sun could heat up if it were cold?

No, it is obvious, and in the same way not even you can love without giving yourself love, without living immersed, or immersed, in this wonderful emotion.

What the experts who recommend only taking care of you seem not to understand is that love is the best possible self-care.

I'll tell you very clearly: more love, more by love, as this love is unconditional, the more you will be happy.

And remember that you can't lose yourself if you don't learn to appreciate who you are and get to know yourself better.

Tell me, how could you take care of yourself better than this?

Remember: awareness is important, but without action nothing will change.

START TO LOVE

Are you suffering from your relationship?

Do you always live the same situations in love?

I will be honest with you: you will continue to suffer and the fault is yours alone!

If you don't act right away, you will continue to suffer...

The 3 reasons that prevent you from stopping suffering in love

We would all like to be happy in love, we would all like to live an exciting life full of moments to remember, but the reality is another:

The majority of people are not happy in love

Look around: friends, relatives, acquaintances and tell me how many happy people do you see?

How many people satisfied with their relationship and more generally with their life do you know?

Of course, we all would like to experience these emotions and be happy, but why do few people succeed?

There are 3 behaviors, three actions that we should do and that we neglect, that prevent people, and probably you too, from getting what they want.

If you don't act following these 3 behaviors you will not be able to live a healthier and happier life, love and relationship.

You will not be able to stop suffering

1. Focus on what you can really change

Imagine the life of each person as contained in two large spheres: a large and a smaller one.

One sphere more external and the other that is inside.

The bigger one represents everything that revolves around your life, but over which you have no control.

International political decisions, wars, world hunger, global pollution, partner decisions, thoughts of friends and relatives, dreams and hopes of those you know , your boss and all that others think and do.

All things that in some way intertwine with your life, people and facts that involve you, but that you cannot concretely direct or influence.

Can you control your partner like a puppet?

Can you choose and influence his thoughts or behaviors?

Can you solve the problem of world hunger or stop wars and environmental pollution?

You can't. None of us can do that.

Likewise, you cannot decide what your partner should do and think.

You cannot program him to behave in a certain way or as you wish. You are unable to change who he is as a person, his values and beliefs.

The other sphere, the smaller one, represents your most intimate world. In this sphere they are enclosed all things, facts and possibilities on which you have direct control instead.

They are all those situations that you can influence with your thoughts and behaviors

At the center of this sphere are you. The only person you can influence in a strong and concrete way is yourself.

You can decide what to do and what not to do, you can work on your thoughts and you can change your behaviors and decide your actions.

You can influence your life in every single aspect, from every angle.

You can follow your values and make your own decisions, which will change your world more or less incisively.

You can choose to love you more and not allow others to make you the bad and make you suffer, you can choose to behave differently with your partner, with your boss, with your friends and relatives.

You can work on yourself and in this way your personal sphere will start to get bigger.

The more you direct your choices and take responsibility for them, the more your personal sphere grows and becomes stronger. The more you work on yourself, the more your world changes.

The first problem is just that: the things you focus on

Too often we are led to wait for solutions that come from the outside. We want others to work things out for us.

"If he would stop, if he behaved in another way, if he said this and did this, if if ... then I could stop suffering"

If all this happens then you will be happy and stop suffering, but this is unlikely to happen if you don't work to change things.

What to do:

If you really want your life and relationship to change, if you want to experience love in a productive way of happiness, if you want to understand how to stop suffering, then you no longer have to wait for someone to take action to change things for you.

You have to stop focusing on the outside and all those things and situations that you have no control over, but you have to start focusing on what YOU can do.

Whenever you are faced with something that makes you feel bad or that bothers you , ask yourself what YOU can do to change the situation.

Focus on the solution instead of focusing on the problem or shifting the responsibility to others.

Ask yourself what you can and must do to be happy if you are not, what YOU can do to live a love and a healthy relationship, what YOU can do to avoid being humiliated and hurt, what YOU can do to stop living the situations that make you feel bad.

The very moment you start focusing on yourself, taking responsibility for changing your relationship and your life, then you will really start to change things.

2. Accept fear and don't just see the negative

Whenever you think about changing something important in your life, you are afraid.

Fear and dread of change are a constant in many choices.

Of course, in fact, those that do not scare you are choices that do not serve to change things.

Always remember that choices that don't grab your stomach and squeeze it tightly are decisions that won't change your life in any way.

Deciding to change things is scary.

I know this well and it is a normal reaction, just as I know it is not easy, but I also know that it can be done: fear can be faced and overcome.

How many times have you been afraid in your life?

Fear of changing jobs, driving a car, facing an exam or learning to ride a bicycle and then maybe you realized that they were just limiting beliefs and that it wasn't as bad as it seemed?

The problem is that we are very good at focusing on everything that can go wrong, while also being able to invent and create possibilities that do not exist.

This way you are only feeding fear.

"If he lets me what I'll do, how can I live without him. I will not find another man and I will be alone. Better him than someone I don't know, at least I already know his faults. "

All of these fears prevent you from being happy. They immobilize you and fill your head with demons that seem invincible to you.

What to do:

You are scared? Look in the mirror and tell yourself that this is perfectly normal. We are all afraid.

Instead of focusing on what could go wrong, shift your focus to everything that would change for the good in your life if you made that choice.

"If I end this relationship, I will finally be able to stop suffering and feel bad and I can start living again. "I'll find another man who loves and respects me because I deserve   to   be   happy." "If I still allow him to treat me this way, I can never be truly happy"

The moment you begin to see the other side of the coin, things will appear to you in a different light.

When you understand that every choice can also bring positive results then you will be ready to face and overcome fear.

In that precise moment you will understand how to stop suffering and start living a new life.

Always remember that brave people are not the ones who are not afraid, but they are the ones who face and overcome their fears.

3. Take action: change your habits

Too often it is thought that to change things you have to make who knows what great gestures, but in reality this is not the case.

Have you ever tried to go on a diet? Remove all of a sudden, bread, pasta, sweets and a whole range of foods that you are used to eating?

How much effort did you go through and how long did it last? The motivation was strong, yet how many times have you given up or regained the lost pounds?

All this happens because changing habits is really hard.

Even a relationship, however difficult or disastrous it is, creates habits that we struggle to let go of.

How many people do you know who have painful emotional relationships but do nothing to change their situation?

It sounds absurd, but these people have gotten used to suffering and are afraid of facing something new.

They are afraid to give up their habits, however painful they may be and create happier new ones.

We often know very well how to stop suffering, but we choose to remain in our swamp of suffering.

We prefer to continue to experience a known pain, rather than move to find something different that makes us feel better and allows us to smile again.

If you don't become aware that some habits you have are harmful to your happiness, you will hardly be able to live a healthy love.

"He is like that, by now I'm used to the way he treats me, I'm used to his outbursts or the fact that he doesn't consider me. I'm used to this life and its betrayals"

All these behaviors you are addicted to will not allow you to experience the love you desire.

These habits will not allow you to be happy and they will not allow you to change things.

I want to be brutally honest: nothing will ever change until you're TU to change.

If you do not from the make and start to act by changing your relational habits will not change anything in your life.

What to do:

Take your time. Don't think you can change all the things you don't like in one fell swoop, but even if you slowly start acting NOW.

Focus on what you want and ask yourself what you can do to change things. Stop accepting passively and with a sense of resignation everything you don't like.

Do you repress your emotions? Does he not listen to you? Do everything for him, do you feel bad and don't know what to do?

Start talking, talk about what you are feeling, take the time, but don't hope that it only takes one to change things.

You have to continue, go on and insist until talking, taking time or expressing your emotions clearly, have become new and healthy habits for you.

Over time, everything that now seems like an effort will become something normal.

One day you will wake up and have replaced all those habits that made you feel bad, with others that will improve your life.

One step at a time with constancy and perseverance and one morning you will realize that things are really changing.

It is important not to stop, but to act constantly, because you never know when things could change.

Now you know the reasons why you will never be happy in love if you don't take responsibility for changing things.

Now you know how to stop suffering and start living love in a healthy way:

Change your thoughts; focus on what YOU can do to get what you want.

Take responsibility without waiting for your partner to do something for you or for a miracle to happen.

Accept fear as a normal life emotion. Fear that manifests itself strongest when you are doing something that can really change your life.

Change your habits, take action. Every day you take one small step, one small change, and in the end you will get huge results.

CONCLUSION

Getting out of an emotional addiction is a path that presents complexities. It is not enough to open the door of the prison in which we lived, we must find the strength and the courage to cross that threshold.

And it's not easy if all around you see only ravines and precipices.

Low self-esteem, lack of trust, lack of love and respect for oneself and the refusal to recognize the need to have one's own place in the world, make up a decidedly inadequate psychological arsenal to face the battle against the monster of fear of abandonment.

The "I can't live without him or her" is a mental burden that has little to do with the extreme romance of certain films. It is a phrase that hides the cry of that inner emptiness that demands only one thing from us: to be scrutinized by the eyes of our conscience.

Below you list a series of reflection with the hope that you can provide that ' input necessary to start a revival path if you find yourself in a situation of emotional dependence. After all , Newton discovered it... "A body in motion tends to remain in motion". The problem with any marathon lies in that damn first step...

1- You need space... your space

You have lost your identity along the way that set of characteristics, virtues and defects that make you a unique example of a race so widespread on this planet. You can find it only within a mental and psychological space where you can perceive boundaries. We are a "one" connected with a "whole". Everything belongs to us when we become aware of what divides us.

2- Your Holy Grail is called.... Autonomy

Your survival, in this psychological case, cannot depend on someone else. In the transition between "being a victim of circumstances" and being the "blacksmith of one's own destiny", the extraordinary encounter between our inside and our outside takes place. The human adventure is completed.

3- Your house is called ... Trust in you the same

The emotional addict lives daily immersed in a drama: the other is both the object of his desire and his greatest fear. His own mental and psychological balance depends on his presence; his greatest terror takes energy from his possible absence. He lives between these two extremes without ever finding his own balance in the middle. A middle point that holds the most precious treasure: the ability to perceive one's own value, regardless of what one has become or what one has obtained.

4- Living on the Surface Means Surviving

There is no other solution, there is no other way. You have to be willing to go deep inside; you have to have the intention of meeting your soul. You have to find the courage to sit next to that disconsolate, hurt and abandoned child to convince him that life is waiting for him. Sometimes the only way to choose which road to take at an intersection is to look back to see where you are coming from.

5- Discovering the Here ... Searching the Now

To get out of an emotional addiction, you have to stop being afraid. To do this you have to be aware of one thing: fear is always an offshoot of the past or a projection into the future. The moment you live and the place you are may not match your wishes, but they remain the most important place and time for you. The one where you can change ... change what you don't like about what you have been and change what scares you about what you might be ...

6- The most sincere friend: Loneliness

Befriend the bitterest of your enemies. Get familiar with loneliness. Face the most feared monster. For the person suffering from emotional addiction it is undoubtedly the hardest step. The step that takes place between the two borders of one's inner precipice. Yet it is the necessary step to discover in one's "death" the only possibility of "rebirth".

7- Return to love each other in order to love others in a healthy way

They instilled it in us as a pleasure to be enjoyed every now and then, but "loving yourself" is a duty to be experienced as a lifestyle. It has been sold to us as the product of selfishness to be taken with a grain of salt but "taking care of you" is the most selfless act we can do. Giving others our happiness, our will to live and our energy is the greatest gift we can give to the world. A necessary contribution for those who live our time. A happy world is made up of happy people. A result that must lead back to a fundamental premise: the world asks you to be happy with him ... not to sacrifice yourself for him!!!

8- Asking for Help Is an Act of Courage

When you are at the bottom of the well, calling someone to stretch a rope to go up may be the best solution. You have to regain confidence with who you are, with your body, with your value, with your identity. Crossing the forest in the company of someone will not prevent you from feeling fear but will give you more courage to continue. Those who look at you from the outside may point out those small improvements that will serve as the foundation for the construction of a new yourself: a person who, on the journey to their own center, will find the desire to face life's challenges.

CPSIA information can be obtained
at www.ICGtesting.com
Printed in the USA
BVHW060032260221
601128BV00005B/262